INDUSTRIAL RESEARCH DEPARTMENT
WHARTON SCHOOL OF FINANCE & COMMERCE
UNIVERSITY OF PENNSYLVANIA

RESEARCH STUDIES
XXXVIII

PHILADELPHIA WORKERS IN A CHANGING ECONOMY

Philadelphia Workers in a Changing Economy

by

Gladys L. Palmer

PHILADELPHIA
UNIVERSITY OF PENNSYLVANIA PRESS

Published in Great Britain, India, and Pakistan by Geoffrey Cumberlege:
Oxford University Press, London, Bombay, and Karachi

MANUFACTURED IN THE UNITED STATES OF AMERICA BY
BOOK CRAFTSMEN ASSOCIATES, INC., NEW YORK

Preface

THIS STUDY PROVIDES a summary of a research program that owed its initial inspiration to a report made to the Mayor of Philadelphia in 1915 by Joseph H. Willits, then of the Wharton School of the University of Pennsylvania. When asked to find out how many unemployed there were in the city and what could be done about the problem, he reported that "the most fundamental fact about unemployment in Philadelphia or any other American industrial center is that we know practically nothing about it." Among other considerations, Mr. Willits stressed the need of record-keeping by employers on hirings and layoffs and by the community on changes in employment and unemployment, if we were ever to come to grips with the problem. The need for continuing information was based on his finding that although unemployment is worse during a depression than in prosperity, it is a chronic phenomenon of modern industry.

In the development of an industrial research program at the Wharton School in 1921, attention was paid to the analysis of labor-market phenomena as well as to other economic and social problems of business. Individual studies emphasized issues that were important at the time. For example, the measurement and analysis of labor turnover, the causes of absenteeism, the use of help-wanted advertising as a barometer of the demand for labor, the potentialities of municipal public works as a device for stabilizing employment, seasonal patterns of factory employment, and the methods by which workers find jobs, all constituted subjects of study and reports to the public in the years from 1921 to 1932. Beginning in 1929, annual population sample surveys were initiated to provide a continuing series of data on the work status of the Philadelphia labor force and the size and nature of its unemployment problem. This program was continued to 1938 in cooperation with several community agencies. With the assistance of the WPA National Research Project in 1936 and 1937, the annual surveys were supplemented by studies of the activities of public employment offices, the mobility of workers in selected occupations of importance in the city, and the relation of unemployment to public relief programs. In cooperation with the Bureau of the Census, several labor-force surveys were made during World War II, using the improved sampling techniques that had been developed at the Bureau, and emphasizing the recruiting problems of war industries. In 1951, in cooperation with the Bureau of the Census, the Social Science Research Council, and six other university research centers, a survey of labor mobility in a sample of the city's labor force was made as part of a larger program of study sponsored by the U. S. Air Force.

The findings of each of the studies undertaken and their contributions to techniques of labor-market analysis have been summarized elsewhere (see Bibliographical Appendix), but the substantive contribution of the program as a whole has been drawn upon for this report. There is more information for the Philadelphia labor market than for many other cities and to bring together the findings of scattered studies and interpret them in the light of longer-term developments constitutes one reason for the writing of this report.

Research grants from several foundations and the cooperation of national and local public agencies made possible the research program on which this report is based. To the former Directors of the Industrial Research Department of the University of Pennsylvania, Anne Bezanson, Hiram S. Davis, and Joseph H. Willits, and to the staff members who contributed to this program in its early stages, the writer is deeply indebted. Evan B. Alderfer, Hans Blumenfeld, Carol P. Brainerd, Philip M. Hauser, Miriam Hussey, Stanley Lebergott, Herbert S. Parnes, Lloyd G. Reynolds, and George W. Taylor have made many helpful suggestions on the manuscript. The cooperation of the U. S. Bureau of the Census with respect to permission to publish certain data as well as assistance in conducting surveys and on technical matters is gratefully acknowledged. In addition, special mention should be made of the fine assistance of Ann Ratner Miller in the early stages of the development of materials for this report and of June R. Charlamb and Rosamond J. Sanderson in its preparation for publication.

CONTENTS

TABLES

CHARTS

APPENDIX TABLES

PHILADELPHIA WORKERS IN A CHANGING ECONOMY

Chapter I

Introduction

IN THE SEARCH for a pattern of the ebb and flow in any working environment, it is obvious that concurrent elements of stability and change characterize metropolitan labor markets over time. Despite the aspects of a city's population that appear to be enduring, its composition in terms of age, sex, and nationality or race is constantly shifting. Despite a persistence in the long-term economic functions of a city, there are continuing changes in the kinds of goods and services produced, in production processes, in types of business organization, and in the skills of workers. Some of these dynamic forces may appear to be independent of each other, but they usually interact to produce variations in the size and composition of the labor force and in the levels of employment and its distribution by occupation and industry.

Labor-market phenomena may be broadly conceived to include almost all aspects of the economic and social life of a working population, but it is seldom possible to cover such a broad field in one study or series of studies. Emphasis in this report is placed on the structural framework of a metropolitan labor market and its dynamics in terms of changes in the levels and distribution of employment and in the size, composition, and mobility of the labor force. These aspects of the labor market are not appraised from the point of view of the individual firm or worker, or from the point of view of social institutions that influence the operations of the labor market. Rather, the intent is to provide a pattern of the dynamics of a metropolitan labor market that can be used as a basis for subsequent study of the behavior of individuals in the labor market, specific problems in recruiting or training workers, or the effect of institutional forces on job transactions at a particular point in time or on the work experience of individuals over time.

An additional reason for the particular scope of this report is that the economics of cities deserves more attention than it has had from economists. One of the costs of progress in a nation is that some industries decline while others expand and some communities decrease in importance while others gain. Little is known about the processes of adaptation to such changes in a community, although public policy is increasingly directed toward minimizing the need for or the costs of such adaptation. This report therefore examines the experience of Philadelphia to learn directly about labor-force dynamics in a metropolitan community and indirectly about certain aspects of a city's economic development.

Comparisons with other cities and with the nation are introduced from time to time in the analysis, primarily to explain Philadelphia's experience. Since manufacturing is an important part of the economic base in most large cities, considerable emphasis has been placed on trends in the demand for labor in manufacturing industries and on changes in the relative position of this community in the national economy. Both the basic data and the analysis should be useful to economists concerned with specific economic developments in metropolitan areas or with the geographic impact of national influences, to students of labor-market phenomena and community planning problems, and to business, union, and community leaders and workers in the Philadelphia area.

The organization of the information may be briefly summarized at this point. Because of the maturity of Philadelphia as a leading manufacturing center, the character of its industries and labor market was well established many decades ago. An understanding of the emergence of these attributes in the local economy is essential to an appreciation of the significance of more recent changes. This historical background constitutes the subject matter of the next chapter. Chapter III describes changes in the relative position of Philadelphia in the national economy and analyzes in some detail the shifts that have occurred in the demand for labor in recent decades. The characteristics of its business enterprises and their products and other aspects of its economic life are compared with those of other large cities and the significant features of the economic base are highlighted. As a background for more detailed discussion, changes in the size and composition of the population and the labor force from 1910 to 1950 are reviewed in Chapter IV, with a considerable emphasis on comparing national and local trends in the age, sex, and occupational skills of the labor force.

The character and size of the city's unemployment problem during the thirties are discussed in detail in Chapter V for the light they throw on the cumulative effects of a severe and prolonged depression on various aspects of labor-market phenomena in a metropolitan city. The series of data available for Philadelphia during this decade provides insight into the dynamics of the process of employment and unemployment. World War II reversed many of the prewar trends in the economy of Philadelphia and its environs, as in other areas. The experience of the labor force during World War II and postwar years is described in Chapter VI, including analysis of changes in the population and labor force and in the industrial and occupational distribution of employment, the expansion of industrial facilities for war production and later contraction, and concomitant changes in a variety of labor-market indicators.

The interpretation of local events is suggested throughout the analysis, but the concluding chapter summarizes the findings in the broader context of labor-force dynamics in relation to economic change in metropolitan cities. One question that the report attempts to answer concerns the character, intensity, and causes of recent changes in the structure of the local economy. To what extent were local changes paralleled in the nation or in metropolitan cities generally? Did they primarily reflect changes in Philadelphia's competitive position as a center of population and industry relative to more rapid expansion of the nation's population and industry in other regions and industrial areas? Did heavy local concentration of industries that were subject to long-term decline account for major changes in the area's industrial structure? The differentiation of these influences provides clues not only to interpreting Philadelphia's experience but also to understanding the growth patterns of cities and their vulnerability to structural changes in the economy and to variations in the levels of business activity.

A broad field of inquiry closely related to these considerations concerns the flexibility or inflexibility of the labor force in making adaptations to structural changes in an economy. Again, some variations in local labor-force patterns parallel those in the nation or in metropolitan cities generally while others reflect primarily local demographic and economic influences. Is there evidence, for example, that a metropolitan labor force contracts in depression and expands in prosperity? Does migration accompany changes in job opportunities? Is expansion for the most part effectuated by recruiting young workers to jobs or do experienced workers shift from declining to expanding industries? Is there evidence that relatively strong work-attachments to a single employer or other institutional forces, such as employers' hiring practices, impede such adjustments? In other words, is a metropolitan labor force sufficiently mobile to meet changing labor requirements in a local economy and how are the changes accomplished?

Chapter II

The Emergence of Philadelphia as a Manufacturing Center

A BRIEF REVIEW of Philadelphia's economic history, based on secondary sources, indicates that the industrial structure of the city so well established many decades ago has been relatively persistent. What one might call the general industrial characteristics of the community are therefore of long standing. Philadelphia has been and continues to be a diversified manufacturing center, with a relatively high proportion of employment devoted to the production of non-durable goods. Its industries and many of its enterprises are mature and well established in their markets. Population growth has been slow but steady during most of the city's history. Its location on the Atlantic Seaboard attracted many European immigrants and its specialization in certain types of industries brought skilled workers from the European centers of these industries.

The city's contribution to the colonial and early national economy varied with the fortunes of the country and with changes in the location of the population and the character of its economic activities. For nearly a century, Philadelphia was the leading port of the country. Perhaps as a corollary of this position, it became a shipbuilding center, making what came to be regarded as the "crack sailers" of the ocean.[1] In addition to its contribution of many outstanding leaders in the War for Independence, the local area was at times both the "breadbasket" and arsenal for General Washington's Army. Philadelphia merchants, acting as bankers, were often responsible in large part for the financing of the war and the city continued to be

1 Edwin T. Freedley, *Philadelphia and Its Manufactures* (Philadelphia, 1858), p. 76.

the leading banking center of the new republic for several decades after independence was won.

The opening of the Erie and Champlain Canals diverted traffic to the West from Philadelphia to New York, and the commercial facilities of New York eventually drew foreign trade from the port of Philadelphia.[2] New York City soon took the lead as the most populous city and "by about 1830 had also wrested from Philadelphia the distinction of being the leading financial center of the country."[3] The loss of foreign trade was attributed by one writer to the withdrawal of local capital from foreign trade to the industrial and mining development of Pennsylvania.[4] He goes on to say that:

> . . . in all probability I would not misrepresent popular feeling if I were to say that Philadelphia does not covet the distinction of being a great importing mart. She would be content if other cities monopolized the doubtful honor of importing hither French gimcracks and German cloths in exchange for gold or silver . . . provided her merchants were encouraged to devote their energies successfully and uninterruptedly to building up Home Industry and American Manufactures.[5]

Although this quotation may reflect a jaundiced feeling about the rising star of New York, there is no doubt but that the city's attention was increasingly drawn to the exploitation of Pennsylvania's coal and iron resources and to the development of manufactures.

Early Leadership in Manufacturing

Manufactures had had an early start in Philadelphia. Writing in 1794, Tench Coxe estimated that one-fourth of the adult male population of Philadelphia and its suburbs was engaged in manufactures.[6] Coxe cites the development of spinning mills, paper mills, gunpowder mills, steel works, rolling mills, shipyards, and book-printing shops.[7] "Philadelphia goods" had a reputation throughout the colonies that

---

2 Chester W. Wright, *Economic History of the United States* (New York: McGraw-Hill Book Co., Inc., 1941), p. 324.

3 *Loc. cit.*

4 Freedley, *op. cit.*, p. 87.

5 *Ibid.*, p. 89.

6 Tench Coxe, *A View of the United States of America* (Philadelphia, 1794), p. 228.

7 *Ibid.*, p. 64.

persisted through the first half of the nineteenth century. In many instances they eventually displaced foreign imports.

The first carpet factory in the country was located in Philadelphia, as was also the first paper mill, and developments of the printing press, calico printing, frame-work knitting, the making of fur-felt hats, and the tanning of leather were initiated in this area prior to the Revolution.[8] By the middle of the nineteenth century, Philadelphia had gained leadership in the nation's iron and steel industry and in a variety of foundry and heavy engineering products, in textile machinery, in paper products, and in the tanning of leather. By 1860, moreover, the city had become the greatest single center of the woolen and hosiery industries, and, "considering all materials and fabrics, Philadelphia remained our leading textile city."[9] It was the home of the largest locomotive works and saw factory in the country, if not in the world. In addition, a substantial production of ships, boots and shoes, apparel, printing and bookbinding, hardware, chemicals, and other products characterized the manufacturing activities of the community.

The city's locational advantages for the production of arms and ships is illustrated in the early establishment of Government facilities in the area. The building of the Philadelphia Navy Yard was authorized in 1798 and the Yard continued in operation until 1862. During the Civil War, the City of Philadelphia acquired League Island which was later given to the Federal Government for operation as a naval base and shipyard and the Island continues to be the location of the Philadelphia Naval Base. The building of the Frankford Arsenal, which also is still in operation, was authorized in 1815.[10] Other types of Government facilities were located here at later dates.

A Skilled Labor Center

The city was a center for skilled craftsmen as well as a proving ground for many types of mechanical inventions and manufacturing

---

8 This paragraph is summarized from Victor S. Clark, *History of Manufactures in the United States* (New York: McGraw-Hill Book Company, Inc., 1929), Vol. I; *Manufactures in the United States in 1860* (Eighth Census); and Freedley, *op. cit.*

9 Clark, *op. cit.*, I, 559.

10 This paragraph was summarized from two volumes of the *American Guide Series* prepared by the WPA Federal Writers' Project: *Philadelphia, A Guide*

processes. "In the invention and construction of machinery and instruments for practical and scientific purposes, Philadelphia mechanics early acquired a reputation for skill."[11] That skilled mechanics from Europe were attracted to this area is attested in the following comment:

> Men who would not go to "Raw Cheney" in Georgia for $1000 a year, nor to Pittsburgh for $900, nor to Lowell for $850 eagerly came to Philadelphia for $800. Philadelphia has thus the pick and choice, at less wages, of the mechanics of the Union. Hence, too, the name PHILADELPHIA MECHANIC has become synonomous with skill and superiority in workmanship. We simply state a well-tested fact when we assert that a mechanic, traveling with favorable credentials from respectable workshops in this city, will be preferred to fill the first vacancy in any similar establishment, not merely in most places throughout the United States, but in portions of Europe.[12]

One historian notes that there was a permanent textile operative class in Philadelphia in the first decades of the Republic and that this labor supply influenced the organization of the textile industry here.[13] The majority of textile workers were English or Anglo-American. Of the Philadelphia women employed as textile workers during this period, it was said that "the female operatives, though perhaps less literary than their Lowell sisters, are seemingly as attractive in appearance, skillful in manipulation, and correct in deportment."[14]

Philadelphia textile industries developed somewhat differently from those in New England. Their organization resembled that of Great Britain, with segregated operations and manufacture to order rather than with integrated operations and quantity production.[15] In this area, spinning, weaving, dyeing, printing, and finishing were usually independent operations. Yarn mills specialized in making specific types of yarns and a variety of subsidiary operations developed around the industries located here. Some hand-loom weaving

---

to the Nation's Birthplace (Philadelphia: William Penn Association, Inc., 1937) and *Pennsylvannia, A Guide to the Keystone State* (New York: Oxford University Press, 1940.)

11 J. L. Bishop, *A History of American Manufactures* (Philadelphia, 1864), p. 576.

12 Freedley, *op. cit.*, p. 73.

13 Clark, *op. cit.*, I, 540.

14 Freedley, *op. cit.*, p. 252.

15 Clark, *op. cit.*, II, 429.

was performed in weavers' homes as late as 1890 in the carpet industry, although in cotton, silk, and woolen and worsted branches most operations had been transferred to the factory by 1860. In all branches of the industry, with the possible exception of hosiery, expansion in this area induced the migration of skilled weavers, designers, and enterprisers from Great Britain. Philadelphia's early leadership in the cotton goods industry was lost to New England centers prior to 1860, but it retained leadership in the woolen and worsted, carpet, and hosiery industries during later decades.[16]

The demand for goods during the Civil War led not only to expansion of the manufacture of textiles, clothing, and boots and shoes, but also to increased activity in local shipyards, engineering works, and machine shops. By 1870, Chester had the largest shipyards in the country and the facilities at Philadelphia, Camden, Chester, and Wilmington made the Delaware Basin the largest shipbuilding center in the country.[17] In referring to the effects of the Civil War and reconstruction periods on local developments, Clark summarized the situation in 1867:

> Philadelphia easily retained its ancient primacy as the leading manufacturing center of the country . . . It was the commercial center of 260 cotton and woolen mills and still had several thousand hand looms, and it contained the largest chemical works, publishing houses, locomotive works and machine shops in the country.[18]

Philadelphia's population has increased slowly but steadily throughout most of its history. In the century from 1790 to 1890, decennial percentage gains ranged from 19 to 45 per cent except in the decade from 1850 to 1860, when substantial territorial additions to the city's corporate limits yielded an unusually high population gain. From 1890 to 1900, however, Chicago took second rank among the largest cities of the country and Philadelphia dropped to third place. This position has been retained, although Detroit and Los Angeles have challenged it more recently. Decennial population gains were relatively lower in the twentieth than in the nineteenth century, particularly after World War I, and between 1930 and 1940

---

16 *Ibid.*, pp. 429-44.
17 *Ibid.*, p. 147.
18 *Ibid.*, p. 146.

the city lost population. A significant part of the city's early growth came from European immigration, while the migration of Negroes from the South was responsible for a substantial part of the later gains.

Despite changes in the relative importance of Philadelphia in the nation and the development of new industries and products over a century and a half, there have been elements of stability in its functional structure. Adequate statistical data are not available to measure the degree of stability or change in all aspects of the city's economic life, but use has been made of certain data for the occupations of heads of families in 1799 and in 1940. (Table 1) Major changes in the materials and products worked on and in the job requirements in specifiic types of occupations had occurred between these two dates, but the distribution of economic activities has striking similarities with respect to broad functions. Its differences reflect a shift from commodity-producing to service industries and from a domestic household economy to the commercialized way of life in modern cities. Changes in factory processes are illustrated in the fact that almost all of the family heads engaged in manufacturing and mechanical pursuits in 1799 were craftsmen, but, by 1940, only a fifth of this total were so classified.

Table 1
INDUSTRY OF FAMILY HEADS
PHILADELPHIA, 1799 AND 1940

Industry group	1799[a]		1940[b]	
	Number	Per cent	Number	Per cent
Total	3,585	100.0	356,780	100.0
Agricultural pursuits	18	0.5	713	0.2
Professional services & government	255	7.1	43,527	12.2
Personal services[c]	679	18.9	37,105	10.4
Trade, transportation, finance	1,117	31.2	128,798	36.1
Manufacturing & mechanical pursuits	1,516	42.3	146,637	41.1

[a] From *A Century of Population Growth*, U. S. Bureau of the Census, 1900, chap. XV, p. 143. Data are for population within city boundaries of 1790 and Southwark.
[b] Estimates by industry group derived from occupational group data (*1940 Census of Population, Families: General Characteristics*, Table 58) to which percentage distributions of industry by occupation for 1940 were applied. Data refer to employed family heads.
[c] Includes amusement and recreation and domestic service in 1940 but probably not in 1799.

STABILITY OF BUSINESS STRUCTURE

In addition to relative stability in its functional structure, there have been elements of constancy in the business structure of the community. A significant number of the outstanding business enterprises that developed manufacturing in the city and its environs in the nineteenth century are in existence today. Although the processes of manufacture and the character of products and markets have changed, individual concerns have continued to manufacture goods in the same type of industry or product-class. When "Old Ironsides" was built in 1832, it was called a "fair weather" locomotive by the public press because the problem of maintaining traction on wet rails had not yet been solved.[19] It took 20 years for the Baldwin Locomotive Works to produce its first 500 engines, but by 1880 it had built 5,000 locomotives.[20] From a congested central city location, the plant expanded in the suburbs and, in 1928, consolidated all operations in its present suburban location. But as early as 1907 locomotives had become so large that it was "all but impossible to get them out of the Philadelphia plant."[21] Steam locomotives, diesel-electric engines, and a wide variety of heavy engineering products are made by the Baldwin Locomotive Works today.

The Whitaker Mill, a small plant producing heavy cotton cloths, such as duck, awning materials, and mattress tickings, was established in 1809 on what was then the outskirts of the city of Philadelphia. All of the stages of the Industrial Revolution in the textile industry are represented in the history of this plant. Weaving was done on hand looms in workers' houses in the early stages of development and the spinning mill was run by water power. Gradually all operations were consolidated in the plant and steam power substituted for water power. The plant is still at the same location, although the city has spread around and beyond it. Moreover, seven generations of the founder's family have continued to manufacture the same kind of cotton goods made there originally, in competition with New England and Southern mills.

The relative stability of business enterprise in the community not only testifies to the ability of outstanding enterprises to meet successfully competition from other centers or from new types of products or processes, but has also had an effect on the character of

---

19 J. Thomas Scharff and Thompson Westcott, *History of Philadelphia, 1608-1884* (Philadelphia, 1884), III, 2256.

20 Clark, *op. cit.*, II, 339-40.

21 Baldwin Locomotive Works, *The Story of Eddystone* (Philadelphia, 1928), p. 10.

the labor-market attachments of workers. When Henry Disston and Sons, Inc., celebrated its 100th anniversary in 1940, a tenth of some 2,500 employees, engaged in producing a wide variety of products in addition to the saws for which the company is famous, had been with the company continuously for 20 years or longer and 5 per cent for 40 years or longer.[22] Meanwhile, this plant had also moved from its central city location to its present one in order to secure the necessary space requirements for heavy operations, and many of its workers had moved with the plant. It is not possible to secure data by which to compare the average length of service of Philadelphia workers with those of other cities on comparable jobs. It appears probable, however, that the job tenure or company attachments of workers tend to be longer than in most cities, by reason of the substantial number of old and established enterprises and the general acceptance by workers and employers of the desirability of long service with one employer.[23]

Some local industries were established or developed with the aid of tariff protection and the community has traditionally supported protective tariff laws, partly because business failures and unemployment followed the lowering of tariff duties in several stages of manufacturing development here. Throughout the history of the nation's manufactures, local enterprises have had to meet the competition of goods from other centers, first from Europe, later from New England, and still later, from the West and the South.

Impact of Depression and Prosperity

Philadelphia's prosperity fluctuated with the ebb and flow of business activity in the nation. Depressed conditions after the close of the Napoleonic Wars, in 1873, and again in 1893 attracted the

[22] *The Philadelphia Inquirer,* May 25, 1940.

[23] Some evidence in support of this position may be cited from a sample study of the work histories of persons who were 25 years of age or over and at work in 1951 in four cities. The average length (in months) of all civilian jobs held by such workers during the decade 1940-1950 was as follows:

	Philadelphia	Chicago	Los Angeles	San Francisco
Men	51.3	46.3	34.5	38.9
Women	50.3	37.9	30.0	36.7

The average duration of jobs was higher in Philadelphia than in tne other three cities in all age groups from 25 to 55 years, at which point the average duration of jobs for Chicago and Philadelphia workers was the same. At age

most comment in contemporary sources, judging from the fragmentary data still available. *Niles Register,* for example, reported for 1819 that 20,000 persons (out of a population of approximately 64,000) were daily seeking work in Philadelphia.[24] Other sources commented on the layoffs that followed the influx of European goods at this time.[25] Subsequent to these years of unemployment, there were intermittent periods of prosperity and depression. Over several decades, there was a persistent decline in the prices of those goods of which the production was being transferred from the household to the factory and, hence, in the wages of handicraft workers. The desperate condition of hand-loom weavers in Philadelphia, earning $2.50 a week in 1846,[26] was noted in these words: "The squalid poverty which surrounds their miserable homes, their ragged, haggard-looking wives and children, are enough to move the stones themselves."[27]

During the depression of 1857-1858, demonstrations by unemployed workers were responsible for the initiation of public works as a local relief measure. Ward relief committees were developed and a local program began to encourage migration to the West.[28] In the depression that precipated the closing of the Philadelphia banking house of Jay Cooke and Company in September 1873, unemployment continued as a major community problem for several years. Local annual expenditures for outdoor relief amounted to over $500,000, and public feeling was strongly divided on the need for such expenditures.[29] The haphazard distribution of private charity and the demeaning or pauperizing effects of methods of handling public outdoor relief led to the development of organized social

65 there were no significent differences between Chicago, San Francisco, and Philadelphia workers.—Unpublished data from the Survey of Patterns and Factors in Labor Mobility, 1940-1950, which was summarized in Gladys L. Palmer, *Labor Mobility in Six Cities* (New York: Social Science Research Council, 1954).

24 Cited by David Joseph Saposs in John Rogers Commons and Associates, *History of Labor in the United States* (New York: MacMillan Co., 1921), I, 135.

25 Scharff and Westcott, *op. cit.*, III, 2234.

26 Clark, *op. cit.*, I, 396.

27 Cited in John Rogers Commons and Associates, *A Documentary History of American Industrial Society,* VIII (Cleveland: The Arthur H. Clark Co., 1910), p. 237.

28 Leah Feder, *Unemployment Relief in Periods of Depression* (New York: Russell Sage Foundation, 1936), pp. 34-35.

29 *Ibid.*, p. 46.

work agencies—the Germantown Relief Society in 1873 and the Society for Organizing Charity in 1879. The Germantown Relief Society was the first agency in the United States to follow now generally accepted principles governing such organizations.[30] In 1873 as in 1857, local ward associations handled emergency relief activities on a basis of frequent home-visiting and the distribution of relief in kind.[31]

Estimates of the numbers of unemployed Philadelphians in the depression of 1893 range from 50,000 to 62,500 (out of a population of over one million).[32] These estimates are open to question on technical grounds and are undoubtedly understated. A conference, called by the Mayor of Philadelphia in October 1893 "to consider facilities available to care for the unemployed in the Kensington mill district" (a textile district), turned over the administration of unemployment relief to a Citizen's Permanent Relief Committee that had been organized in 1878 to raise funds for various types of emergencies. Home relief was given to 17,908 Philadelphia families representing 71,630 persons. In addition, work relief was provided to 6,000 persons and work relief wages were based on the budgetary needs of families. The facilities of Wayfarers' Lodges for homeless men were extended to women and children. The (Philadelphia) Society for Organizing Charity and other social work agencies participated in this emergency program and it was well organized along modern lines.[33] This scale of emergency relief programs was not again approached in Philadelphia or elsewhere until the depression of 1929 to 1933,[34] when all of the arguments for work relief versus home relief and for or against the need for substantial amounts of public aid were aired again.

The effects of prosperity on the city's economic life are more difficult to trace, perhaps because prosperity is taken in stride and only adversity stimulates comment. Periods of high employment and rising wages occurred intermittently during the nineteenth century, and, as one would expect, were likely to be most spectacular during

30 *Ibid.*, pp. 59, 61.

31 *Ibid.*, pp. 63, 64.

32 *Ibid.*, pp. 77-80. According to one contemporary survey, the number of Philadelphians on relief in the winter of 1893-94 exceeded the numbers in any other large city.—*The Evening Bulletin* (Philadelphia), February 6, 1941.

33 Feder, *op. cit.*, pp. 101-5, 167. The time-period for this program is not stated.

34 *Ibid.*, p. 352.

wars. The Napoleonic Wars, the War of 1812, the Civil War, and the Franco-Prussian War all brought orders for goods to Philadelphia. In fact, the origin of many of the city's industries can be traced to the demand for munitions and military supplies and to the active encouragement of local enterprise to meet this demand.

Fragmentary evidence portrays the characteristic of the labor market that we have come to associate with war and postwar periods. During the Civil War, for example, women employed at the Frankford Arsenal sent a deputation to President Lincoln to secure "government rates on contract work."[35] The average number of wage earners on the payroll of a Delaware River shipyard tripled and quadrupled during the war as compared with prewar levels, and labor turnover was double or triple the prewar rate (which was very high by recent standards.) Hourly earnings in the shipyard moved up from an average of 10 cents in 1854-1857 to 17 cents by the beginning of 1865.[36] Clark comments that after the Civil War large numbers of half-trained workers, imperfectly qualified as machinists, were discharged from army gun-shops and private arsenals.[37] By the time of the Civil War, therefore, all of the symbols of a tight wartime labor market were to be found, namely, labor unrest, rising wages, high labor turnover, and the use of inexperienced workers to expand the labor force. After the war was over, the latter had some difficulty in securing jobs comparable to those held during the war.

Early Philadelphia Labor Movement

Recurring depressions and the economic uncertainties resulting from technological changes brought insecurity of employment and income to workers. Changes in monetary policy added to fluctuations in prices and the cost of living. These conditions, in turn, led to the organization of workers for mutual aid in bargaining with employers, in protecting their civil rights, and in improving their social and economic status. Philadelphia workers were leaders and experimenters in the early labor movements of the nation because this city had

35 *Fincher's Trades' Review*, April 29, 1865, p. 86.

36 Anne Bezanson, "Some Historical Aspects of Labor Turnover" in *Facts and Factors in Economic History* (Cambridge: Harvard University Press, 1932), pp. 696-705.

37 Clark, *op. cit.*, II, 144.

the largest concentration of factory workers as well as a group of craftsmen who had roots in the industrial life of the community. Professor Commons and his associates, in their analysis of the history of the nation's labor movements, identify the first authentic organization of a single trade in a strike of Philadelpia printers in 1786 (for a minimum wage of $6 a week), the first formal collective bargaining negotiations in a contract negotiated by Philadelphia Journeymen Cordwainers in 1799, the first affiliation of a number of trade unions into a central organization for a city in the Mechanics' Union of Trade Associations in Philadelphia in 1827, the first labor party in the Working Men's Party of 1828, and the first labor paper of which any copies have been preserved in the *Mechanics' Free Press*, also of this city.[38]

Early craft unions ran afoul of the English common law doctrine of conspiracy under which several local unions were prosecuted. The testimony in "The trial of the Boot and Shoemakers of Philadelphia, on an Indictment for a Combination and Conspiracy to Raise their Wages" in 1806 presents arguments for and against the practices of trade unions that sound curiously familiar to followers of recent arguments concerning certain provisions of the Taft-Hartley Law.[39] In addition to technical evidence on the issue at stake, more general arguments were introduced concerning the relation of this issue to the position of Philadelphia as a manufacturing center, arguments that have also echoed through subsequent decades. Testimony for the prosecution, for example, noted the quantity of manufactured goods which were exported and the need to support such manufacturing. Union activity would force industries to leave the city. The defense averred that if workers could get better wages in competitive cities like New York or Baltimore, Philadelphia manufacturers would lose their laborers and journeymen and the city would suffer a premature old age.[40]

The boot and shoemakers lost their case, but craft unions continued to spring up in one trade after another. There were numerous local strikes in the period from 1822 to 1840 on issues of wages and hours, as well as agitation against imprisonment for debt and the

38 Commons *et al.*, *History of Labor*, I, 25, 121, 186, 189, 195.
39 Commons *et al.*, *A Documentary History*, III, 59-248, *passim.*
40 *Ibid.*, pp. 136-37.

Pennsylvania militia system and in favor of free schools. The question of whether the labor movement should go into politics or confine itself to collective bargaining activities had been extensively discussed in the late twenties, tried out in local political campaigns, and abandoned after the defeat of the Workingmans' Party in 1831.[41] The Philadelphia General Strike of 1835 saw unskilled coal dock workers, house painters, bricklayers, masons, plasterers, hod carriers, carpenters, blacksmiths, plumbers, leather curriers, cordwainers, printers, auger makers, saddlers, drygoods store clerks, bakers, and city employees uniting in a demand for a ten-hour day. The success of this strike led to a wave of largely successful strikes in other American cities.[42]

By 1836, some 50 craft unions or local organizations of workers were affiliated with the Trades' Union of the City and County of Philadelphia, comprising more than 10,000 members.[43] This organization had been started in 1833 as the result of an appeal from cotton mill operatives in Manayunk.[44] It was in the following year that we find the first record of a strike against wage reductions introduced to enable a local textile mill owner to compete with mills in other areas. The position of the textile strikers in 1834 has been duplicated on many occasions since that time:

> Resolved that as we presume the reasons for Messrs. J. Borie and Company's not being able to pay the old wages for their work to be on account of their machinery not being of the same quality as their competitors in the market, we would recommend to the immediate procuring of new machinery, that they may be able to meet their competitors in the cotton market without oppressing their workmen by reducing their wages.[45]

The scope and intensity of the social ferment that characterized labor's activities in urban centers in the 1830's was not paralleled until a century later. Most of the unions in individual trades and the organizations of more than one trade were short-lived, here as else-

41 Commons *et al.*, *History of Labor*, I, 214-15.

42 Leonard Bernstein, "The Working People of Philadelphia from Colonial Times to the General Strike of 1835," *The Pennsylvania Magazine*, July 1950, pp. 336-39.

43 Commons *et al.*, *A Documentary History*, V, 326.

44 Commons *et al.*, *History of Labor*, I, 374.

45 *The Pennsylvanian*, June 9, 1834, "Resolutions of a public meeting of the working people formerly in the employ of the Schuylkill Factory Company."

where in the nation, although from time to time there were substantial and active movements. In 1865, for example, 42 local unions were listed in a newspaper directory.[46] Philadelphia workers were active also in later national movements, such as the Knights of Labor, in the 1880's. With the turn of the century, unions affiliated with the American Federation of Labor secured a permanent foothold in the local building, printing, and textile industries and other scattered trades. Nevertheless, as in most cities, the majority of Philadelphia's factory workers were not permanently organized into labor unions until after the depression of 1929-1933.

Major Influences in Philadelphia's Early Development

This brief review of phases of the economic history of Philadelphia has emphasized only those aspects of the city's economic activities and its workers that are related to more recent developments to be discussed in subsequent chapters. It was early in the nineteenth century that Philadelphia began to share with New York the servicing of the nation and especially the Middle Atlantic States in transportation and finance, although it retained leadership in manufacturing until a later date. Because of its early start in manufacturing, all stages of the Industrial Revolution are represented in the history of one or another of its industries. The city became a proving ground for early experiments in the labor movement as well as for the transfer of the production of goods from home to factory or the development of new products and processes.

Depressions and wars highlighted the economic trends of the area. Wars introduced into the local economy new industries, which instead of dissolving at the end of the emergency secured a permanent foothold in the city's industrial life. Depressions focused attention on industries in which economic changes were taking place that threatened the competitive position of Philadelphia enterprises. Although there were modifications in the economic structure of the community, its basic industrial pattern changed relatively slowly.

The historical evidence implies that despite the diversity of its manufacturing activities, Philadelphia was extremely vulnerable to depressions and its experience in this respect warrants further exami-

[46] *Fincher's Trades Review,* November 1, 1865.

nation. Local business enterprises and the community's labor force made successful adaptations to a long series of technological and other economic changes as the national economy expanded in other regions and developed new functions. For well over a century, the city's businessmen and industrial workers had to meet competition from new centers, from new types of goods, or from new methods of processing materials. Their success in maintaining Philadelphia's industrial standing among the nation's largest cities in more recent decades is the subject matter of the following chapter.

Chapter III

Changes in the Demand for Labor in Recent Decades

JUST AFTER World War II, Philadelphia and its environs constituted the fourth largest manufacturing area in the nation, as measured by the volume of factory employment. It was surpassed only by the New York, Chicago, and Detroit areas. Basically, the economy of the area[1] now depends on its manufacturing industries, which are diversified in character, and on its importance as a regional shipping and trade center. The Philadelphia port vies with the ports of Baltimore and New York, although most local port traffic prior to World War II was coastwise shipment of petroleum products. The city is also an important center for transportation of coal from the mines of Pennsylvania, agricultural products from a rich farm hinterland, and factory products from a highly industrialized surrounding region.

Although Philadelphia is usually considered a competitor of the largest industrial cities, its manufacturing industries actually compete with those in both large and small communities. This is because its factory products are varied and its enterprises, in many cases, highly specialized. Its textile mills are in competition with plants in New England and the South; its metal products plants with New England and Midwestern plants; its clothing shops with those of

[1] Data for several "areas" are used in this report. The city of Philadelphia is coterminous with Philadelphia County. The Philadelphia Five-County Area includes the counties of Bucks, Chester, Delaware, Montgomery, and Philadelphia. The Eight-County or Standard Metropolitan Area includes the above five Pennsylvania counties as well as Burlington, Camden, and Gloucester Counties in New Jersey. The Delaware Valley or "Greater Philadelphia" Area includes the above eight counties and Mercer and Salem Counties in New Jersey and Newcastle County in Delaware.

New York, Boston, Baltimore, Rochester, Chicago, and St. Louis; its oil refineries with those in other seaboard centers; and its printing and publishing establishments with both small and large cities.

In describing recent changes in the demand for labor, several considerations need emphasis. The first is a change in relative position of Philadelphia after 1890 among the five largest cities both in population and industrial growth. Subsequent discussion analyzes the character of local enterprise, factors in the competitive position of the city and its environs, and changes in the demand for factory labor in the nation and area. Emphasis is placed on trends in the specific segments of manufacturing industry that are relatively important in the local economy. Data are not available for a similar analysis of trends in the demand for labor in nonmanufacturing industries, but use is made of data from the Censuses of Population to indicate developments in this segment of the economy, and recent changes in the local distribution of total employment are compared with national developments. Comparisons are also made with other cities of over 500,000 population in 1950.

Loss of Relative Position among the Five Largest Cities after 1890

The year 1890 marks a major shift in the relative importance of Philadelphia to the national economy and reflects the rise of Midwestern cities to a position of increasing importance. By that date, the center of the iron and steel industry had moved westward from the Atlantic Seaboard and other branches of the metal products industries expanded in the East North Central States. Loss of leadership in an industry implied a loss of relative position in the national economy as the population moved westward and industry expanded in other regions. As will be shown subsequently, however, manufacturing activity continued to increase in this area although at slower rates of growth and Philadelphia continued to retain its early leadership in certain branches of the heavy metal products industries, in textiles, and in the tanning of leather.

The changes that took place in the relative position of Philadelphia in the national economy from the middle of the nineteenth century are indicated by data from the Census of Manufactures on the ratio of Philadelphia's production to that of the nation from 1859 to 1939 in terms of the value of manufactured products. This percentage fluctuated between six and seven from 1859 to 1889. In 1889, it dropped to 4.6 and continued declining until, in 1939, it was 2.5.[2]

In 1880, the populations of New York and Philadelphia outnumbered those of the other three largest cities in the nation by substantial margins. (Appendix Table 1) By 1890, however, Chicago had surpassed Philadelphia. At that time, Detroit and Los Angeles were still small. With other cities, they made substantial population gains during World War I, but they did not pass the million mark until 1930. By 1940, they were closer to Philadelphia's level. Over the period 1880-1930, Philadelphia gained in population but at a declining rate of growth. Los Angeles has made the most spectacular gains of any of these cities, although all five have had periods of rapid population growth. (Appendix Table 2)

Since recent economic developments in the country as a whole and in the Philadelphia area are closely tied to the developments in manufacturing industries, trends in the over-all demand for factory workers are important barometers of economic development. (Appendix Table 3)[3] In the country as a whole, factory wage jobs in 1919 were almost double the number in 1899 and, in 1947, had increased another 40 per cent over the levels of 1919. The demand for factory labor in 1933 reached the lowest point since 1904.

In general, wars have led to the most substantial increases in factory employment only to be followed by substantial declines in postwar years. Peacetime expansion has, for the most part, been less rapid in Philadelphia than in the other large industrial areas. From 1899 to 1914, for example, all of the five largest industrial areas except Philadelphia gained in factory employment at a higher rate than in the nation as a whole. During World War I, the Philadelphia, Los Angeles, and Detroit areas gained more rapidly than the New York and Chicago areas and than the nation. If one disregards the experi-

---

2 The data on the value of product are not adjusted for changes in coverage from census to census. Data on value added by manufacture indicate a further decline in the relative position of Philadelphia from 2.7 per cent of the nation's total in 1939 to 2.4 per cent in 1947.

3 These data exclude employment in government productive establishments. See footnotes to table for coverage adjustments.

ence after World War II in this relatively long span of years, the peaks of factory employment levels in the five largest industrial areas were reached in or immediately after World War I (1919) in the New York and Philadelphia areas, and in 1937 in the Chicago, Detroit, and Los Angeles areas.

Spectacular growth of the automobile industry and the rise of the aircraft industry in recent years explain the later peaks of employment in Detroit and Los Angeles, where these industries are heavily represented. The nation's dependence on New York and Philadelphia for shipbuilding and munitions production during World War I explains high employment levels in 1919 in these areas. It is noteworthy, however, that the Chicago area maintained the gains it made during World War I throughout the next decade, reaching a peak in 1929 and a second peak in 1937, while New York and Philadelphia did not reach 1919 levels again until World War II.

Character of Factory Products

The industrial pattern of manufacturing in the city and its environs is highly diversified. In 1939, manufacturing plants in the Philadelphia Area were reported in 87 per cent (386) of the 446 industry classifications used by the Census of Manufactures. The city's plants were reported in 352 classifications. About 41 per cent of the city's factory employment in 1950 could be classified as in durable goods and 59 per cent in nondurable goods. The ratio of employment in nondurable to durable products is somewhat higher in the city than in its environs, and there is evidence that the predominance of nondurable goods has shown a slow but steady increase since World War I.

Many of the area's products are not end products but are shipped for further processing. Of the final products made in the durable goods industries, many are for industrial use, such as ball bearings, gears, pulleys, machinery, machine tools and equipment, engine parts, construction and transportation equipment, electrical equipment, and measuring instruments. In nondurable goods industries also, a significant part of the work is in processing goods that are sold to industrial users, of which tanned leather, woolen and worsted yarns and goods, dyeing and finishing, upholstery goods, and paper boxes and containers are good examples. Some of the final consumers' goods produced in the area are luxury commodities, such as fine quality fur-felt hats, confectionery, luggage, pianos, jewelry, interior decorating fabrics, and lace. These products are sold in a national market and the prosperity of the industries concerned is heavily dependent on national prosperity. As indicated in the preceding chapter, the area has been noted for "quality" products in a variety of consumers' goods and its heavy industries have supplied the wherewithal for waging a war or for the expansion of manufacturing, mining, construction, communications, or transportation in this country and abroad.

The area has surprisingly few completely integrated enterprises that carry a product through all processes from the raw material to the finished goods. On the contrary, many enterprises are themselves highly specialized or service other specialized activities. In the textile industries, for example, there are yarn mills producing certain grades of yarn, and dyeing and finishing plants and weaving mills similarly specialized. There are also textile machinery plants, textile-equipment repair shops, shops that cut jacquard cards, and designers and chemists who service only textile activities. Similar specialization of activities is found in the metal-fabricating industries, which range from gray iron foundries, steel mills, and plants making heavy industrial machinery to the manufacture of hooks and eyes. Several of the city's industries were, therefore, so organized that the "external economies" of localization and specialization would, in combination, yield the kind of advantages associated with large-scale, integrated enterprises.

The variety of stages of processing and the diversity of products represented in local industries tend to diffuse or minimize the impact of any single economic change and to stagger the effects of business-cycle fluctuations that have a different timing in various industries. However, this does not prevent vulnerability to general tides of prosperity or depression or to changes in marketing arrangements and varying demand in particular consuming industries. Some local textile industries are dependent on high tariff protection and have therefore been affected by changes in tariff legislation. Moreover, dependence on a highly prosperous national or international market or on a war for the kind of expansion that gives prosperity to Philadelphia's heavy industries limits the advantages that might be obtained from another combination of products or from other types of specialization.

Character of Producing Units

Business enterprise in the Philadelphia area tends to be small or moderate in scale. The size is partly the result of the character of the industrial operations located here and partly the result of the type of business organization prevailing at the time many industries were established. For example, in 1939, only a fifth of total manufacturing employment in the area was found in plants employing 1,000 or more persons. (Table 2, Column 8) In Detroit, by contrast, two-thirds of all factory workers were in plants employing 1,000 or more and in Pittsburgh, about one-half. Thirty per cent of factory workers in the Philadelphia area in 1939 were employed in plants with less than 100 and about a half were in moderate-sized plants, employing from 100 to 1,000.[4]

Some differences in the scale of local as compared with national operations by industry may be noted. Local plants tend to employ more workers per unit, on the average, than other plants in the nation in industries producing bread and bakery products, candy, cigars, some types of textile products and apparel, certain chemicals, printing and publishing, and paper products. In the metal industries, on the other hand, except for plants producing tin cans and power-generating equipment, local plants tend to be smaller than those located elsewhere. These differences in size of unit seem persistent and apparently characterized local operations as early as 1910.

There is relatively little employment in the branch plants of large national corporations in this area and in 1941 only 38 per cent of all manufacturing enterprises were conducted by corporations.[5] Many of the corporations doing business in the area are privately owned and the majority of business units are owned by individuals or partnerships. These attributes of business enterprise in the city and area indicate that most business decisions are of local origin for small or moderate-scale operations. The area, therefore, suffers some disad-

4 *1939 Census of Manufactures*, I, 179.

5 Pensylvania Department of Internal Affairs, *Report on Productive Industries, 1939-1941*, p. 58.

vantages from the absence of the financial and technical facilities that are associated with large-scale operations, but has the advantages of closer personal ties between producer and consumer, management and labor, borrower and lender, and business enterprise and the community as a whole.

Historically, much of Philadelphia's business development has been the result of the initiative and leadership of local residents and their families, who built enterprises that have lasted over many decades. In 1950, there were 171 enterprises that had been in business in the area for over 100 years,[6] and a significant proportion of these were manufacturing concerns. A larger number of businesses, in existence for less than a hundred years, have operated for relatively long periods of time. Such well-established enterprises give stability to the structure of business organization in the community.

The roll call of local business enterprises established over a hundred years ago is not germane to this report, but mention of a few firms will indicate the quality of staying-power attributed to business enterprise in the area. In addition to such well-known enterprises as the Baldwin Locomotive Works, the Pennsylvania and Reading railroads, the Lehigh Coal and Navigation Company, Henry Disston and Sons, Inc., the Alan Wood Steel Company, Proctor and Schwartz, and Stephen F. Whitman and Son, Inc., the list includes numerous banks, stores, insurance companies, publishing houses, and journals or newspapers, as well as smaller manufacturing concerns making a wide variety of products.

On the other side of the ledger, some local manufacturing concerns of long-standing national repute in various branches of industry were liquidated in the period between World Wars I and II. In a few instances, these concerns were family estates for which there was apparently no member of the younger generation able or willing to carry on in the family tradition. There is some evidence also that during this period the investments of many family enterprises were increasingly turned away from local to national channels.

All of the general characteristics of local enterprise noted have placed a premium on personal leadership in business at a time when many of the business organizations with which Philadelphia enter-

---

6 *Centenary Business Firms of Philadelphia* (Chamber of Commerce of Philadelphia, 1950).

prises are in competition are increasingly in the form of large corporations operating on a national scale. Some Philadelphia plants became the branch plants of such corporations as they spread over the country, but the general movement in establishment of branch plants has been in the direction of opening new territory in the Southeast, the West, and the Southwest. Large corporations have the financial resources for rapid expansion when opportunities develop.[7] A student of the economic development of California states that much of its industrial development after the depression of 1929-1932 was undertaken in an atmosphere of optimism about increasing population and business prospects on the West Coast and was essentially a national rather than a local development.[8] This type of expansion was one of the contributing factors to a more rapid recovery from the depression in the Los Angeles area, for example, than in the country as a whole and particularly than in an older center like Philadelphia.

Factors in Philadelphia's Current Competitive Position

Many factors contribute to the locational advantages of a city. Its nearness to markets and transportation facilities, the adequacy of its financial resources and other business services, the character of its labor supply, and the size and wealth or income potential of the population in its region all play a part. However, if a city's predominant industries are vulnerable to locational changes, competitive pressures may become severe for the established plants that are usually found in the older manufacturing centers.

For the most part, the so-called "migration of industry" has involved not the physical transfer of equipment and workers but rather the development of new plants in what were considered more favorable locations, as population centers changed and as improved technology freed enterprises from the restrictions of early locations.

7 "Experience indicates that incomes of smaller concerns are typically more sensitive to cyclical swings in business activity, and that as a consequence the relative importance of the largest corporations regularly increases in depressions and is reduced in prosperity."—K. C. Stokes, "Financial Trends of Large Manufacturing Corporations, 1936-1946," *Survey of Current Business*, November 1947, p. 24.

8 F. L. Kidner, *California Business Cycles* (Berkeley and Los Angeles: University of California Press, 1946) p. 116.

The major manufacturing industries that have been characterized by pronounced locational shifts in recent decades have been cotton textiles, hosiery, shoes, iron and steel, rubber tires, and, to a lesser extent, apparel and furniture.[9] Although the movement of the textile industry to the South has perhaps attracted more attention, the long-term westward movement of other industries, notably the durable goods industries, is equally if not more significant. A variety of influences affected these locational shifts, in the opinion of the experts of the National Resources Committee. Changing technology, shifts in the location of major producing units, increasing concentration of production in a few large companies, and considerations of production costs, as well as the movement of population, have caused locational shifts in industry.[10]

From the available evidence, it is not clear to what extent the current competitive position of cities or areas is directly affected by their relative production costs, particularly labor costs. In an analysis of 139 industries between 1929 and 1937, Creamer found that locational shifts had occurred in about half, and these industries accounted for 78 per cent of the factory wage-jobs in 1929. For some industries, the reasons for shifts were indeterminate; for others, technological change or the exhaustion of resources was responsible; and in still others, market and/or cost considerations were predominant factors. Industries that were classified as "labor-oriented" employed about 18 per cent of all factory workers in 1929, and labor-cost differentials were considered to be the chief cause for the locational shifts that occurred in these industries.[11] As a center of the production of certain relatively high labor-cost goods, such as hosiery and other specialized textile products, employment in the Philadelphia area was adversely affected by changes in the location of these industries. Labor-cost differentials played some part in this development but were by no means the exclusive consideration in the loss of competitive position of Philadelphia textile plants.

9 National Resources Committee, *Structure of the American Economy*, Part I, a report made under the direction of Gardiner C. Means (Washington, 1939), p. 58.

10 *Ibid.*, pp. 58-59.

11 Daniel Creamer, "Shifts of Manufacturing Industries," chap. 4 in National Resources Planning Board, *Industrial Location and National Resources* (Washington, 1942).

In its analysis of the structure of the American economy in 1939, the National Resources Committee found that three-fourths of all manufacturing activity is relatively "foot-loose" and that industries are increasingly oriented in terms of market rather than cost considerations.[12] All cities would therefore appear to be in competition for the location of industry, either directly or indirectly.

In the development of the present geographic structure of manufacturing, cities and their environs have played a very important part. The proportion of the total population living in the 33 largest industrial cities and their environs has grown steadily as manufacturing has become more important in the national economy. Despite an increase in plant locations on the periphery of cities as compared with their centers and some industrial expansion in small towns and rural communities, the nation has depended upon its major industrial cities for more than half of total factory output, both in war and peace. Military security considerations and new developments in transportation and technology may conceivably modify this geographic pattern in the future.

It was noted in the preceding chapter that despite its apparent attractiveness to skilled labor, Philadelphia was known to pay lower wages than other cities. The cost of living was generally lower here than in New York City or in western cities, although possibly not lower than in New England. Examination of the fragmentary historical data available on wages in large cities lends support to the view that Philadelphia has continued to be a moderate-wage center.[13] During war periods, the wage ranking of the city has risen, chiefly as the result of shifts of workers from low-wage to high-wage industries such as shipbuilding and munitions.[14] In peacetime, the industrial composition of employment in Philadelphia is weighted in favor

---

12 National Resources Committee, *op. cit.*, pp. 36, 85-104, *passim.*

13 Of the five cities—Chicago, Detroit, New York, Philadelphia, and San Francisco—Philadelphia was in 3rd or 4th place in hourly rates for machinists from 1890 to 1912 and in 5th place for compositors of newspaper work (day) in 1910.—U. S. Bureau of Labor Statistics, Bulletin No. 604, *History of Wages in the United States from Colonial Times to 1928*, pp. 353-54, 305. In a study of selected occupations in the machinery and electrical equipment industry in 1942, Philadelphia's hourly earnings ranked in 3rd, 4th, or 5th place among the above cities for most occupations.—U. S. Bureau of Labor Statistics, mimeographed table dated November 19, 1942.

14 When the 18 largest cities in the country (excluding Washington, D. C.) are ranked from high to low for the average wage per factory wage earner, Phila-

of low-wage rather than high-wage industries. For comparable types of jobs, the wage scales appear to be intermediate in rank, as compared with other large cities.[15] Perhaps as a result, Philadelphia tends to have a high proportion of families with more than one worker per family, and its relative ranking among large cities is higher for family than for individual income.

The city's position with respect to wages takes on greater significance if one realizes that in many of its manufacturing industries labor costs are a relatively high proportion of total costs. Among cities of over 500,000 population, it ranked in seventh place for the ratio of the wage bill to value added by manufacture in 1947. (Table 2) Because of the moderate size and highly specialized character of its factory operations, unionized workers, with few exceptions, do not exert leadership in determining national wage scales or patterns. For example, wage scales in the construction and printing trades here are usually determined after the unions in New York City have set the pattern. Local textile and steel or metal fabricating plants are peripheral to those in other centers and collective agreements are usually made after the national patterns are determined elsewhere. In most of the other industries, predominantly local considerations establish the terms of collective bargaining contracts. This does not mean that the Philadelphia area has no wage disputes or strikes or that trade unions are not important factors in the local economy. On the contrary, the competitive pressures on Philadelphia enterprises make labor costs a vulnerable point of attack and the wage scales developed in local collective agreements constitute an important factor in the maintenance of the competitive position of the area.

Further perspective on the relative position of Philadelphia's industries in the national economy is gained by a comparison of its industrial characteristics with those of other cities of over 500,000 population, excluding Washington, D. C. (Table 2) From this com-

delphia is 15th in 1909, in 8th place in 1919, and in 6th and 5th places, in 1929 and 1939, respectively—*Census of Manufactures*. From 1932 to 1942, the annual average of gross hourly earnings of factory workers was 6 or 7 cents higher in Philadelphia than in the nation as a whole. During the war years from 1942 to 1945, however, this differential increased to between 12 and 14 cents.—Data from Philadelphia Federal Reserve Bank and U. S. Bureau of Labor Statistics.

15 Among 40 labor markets in 1951-52, Philadelphia ranked 27th for wages in clerical jobs and 20th in maintainance jobs.—"Wage Differences among 40 Labor Markets," *Monthly Labor Review*, December 1952, pp. 620-23.

Table 2

SELECTED INDUSTRIAL CHARACTERISTICS OF CITIES OF OVER 500,000 POPULATION EXCLUDING WASHINGTON, D. C.

Cities ranked by population size in 1950	Column 1 Per cent employment in manufacturing to total employment 1950	Column 2 Per cent employment in durable goods to total employment 1950	Column 3 Number of manufacturing industries with locational quotients[a] of 1.50 or over 1950	Column 4 Median family income in 1949	Column 5 Average value added by manufacture per production worker, 1947	Column 6 Ration of wage bill to value added by manufacture, 1947	Column 7 Per cent of women to total employed in manufacturing, 1947	Column 8 Per cent employed in establishments averaging over 1,000 wage-earners in 1939
New York	28.0	8.9	12	$3,526	$7,447	36.7	37.7	11.0
Chicago	36.7	21.7	16	3,956	7,185	39.3	27.5	26.1
Philadelphia	35.1	14.2	16	3,322	6,556	38.8	29.8	21.1
Los Angeles	22.9	12.1	11	3,575	7,047	38.9	25.9	11.8
Detroit	46.0	39.5	3	3,955	6,505	48.0	14.1	64.3
Baltimore	29.0	15.6	12	3,275	6,833	36.4	24.0	29.8
Cleveland	42.4	31.5	10	3,531	7,101	41.3	22.0	25.2
St. Louis	14.4	6.7	15	3,205	6,451	36.9	27.3	17.7
Boston	23.7	9.2	13	3,249	6,870	34.8	33.3	21.3
San Francisco	16.9	7.2	16	3,923	8,588	35.0	22.3	9.0
Pittsburgh	28.2	19.7	10	3,314	6,451	40.7	12.0	50.9
Milwaukee	42.4	27.3	12	3,800	6,956	39.5	22.3	29.1
Houston	20.4	9.4	11	3,389	8,235	32.0	14.2	N.A.
Buffalo	37.3	24.5	11	3,401	7,136	38.3	18.6	26.7
New Orleans	14.2	4.6	15	2,767	5,631	36.8	28.0	N.A.
Minneapolis	24.3	12.8	11	3,784	7,461	33.5	28.3	15.4
Cincinnati	31.6	17.2	14	3,186	6,371	38.7	26.1	15.9
United States	25.9	13.8	—	3,073	6,246	40.6	27.0	22.3

Source: Data in columns 1-4 from *1950 Census of Population*; data in columns 5-7 from *1947 Census of Manufactures*; data in column 7 refer to Standard Metropolitan Areas rather than cities; data in column 8 from *1939 Census of Manufactures* and refer to industrial areas rather than cities.

[a] These locational quotients were computed by dividing the percentage of workers in each of 58 manufacturing industries in a city by the percentage of workers in the same industry in the United States. In this computation the category "not specified manufacturing industries" was omitted.

parison it is clear that Philadelphia is relatively less dependent on manufacturing than Detroit, Cleveland, Milwaukee, Buffalo, or Chicago, but more dependent than the other large cities. Its factory products are predominantly in the category of nondurable goods. The goods produced locally embody a low value added by manufacture and a moderately high labor input, as compared with many large cities. The employment of women is more important to the factories of Philadelphia than to those of the nation or of most of the largest cities. As a corollary of some or all of these attributes, local income levels tend to be low as compared with those in many other metropolitan centers. A comparison of the locational quotients[16] of 58 manufacturing industries for the 17 cities indicates that Chicago, Philadelphia, and San Francisco each have 16 or 17 manufacturing segments that employ at least one and a half times the proportion of workers so employed in the United States as a whole. Detroit and Pittsburgh have the fewest such industries and are, by contrast with Philadelphia, highly specialized manufacturing centers.

The specific industries in which locational quotients for residents of the city and the metropolitan area were high in 1950 are listed in Appendix Table 4. Textiles, apparel, food products, chemicals and oil refining, paper products, leather goods (except footwear), electrical equipment, professional equipment, transportation equipment, and fabricated metal products are all well represented on this list.[17] For various combinations of reasons, these industries have found locational advantages in the city or area of Philadelphia and they constitute the major bulwark of its economic base. The fortunes of some of these industries will be discussed in greater detail subsequently, since their future prospects are important to the continued industrial growth of the community.

Industrial Shifts in the Demand for Factory Labor after World War I

There have been changes in the economic base of Philadelphia over time that are reflected in changes in the demand for labor in

---

16 The locational quotient of an industry expresses a ratio based on its percentage of total employment in a local economy divided by its percentage of total employment in the nation for the same period.

17 A parallel type of computation from the *1947 Census of Manufactures* indicates

different manufacturing industries. For this analysis, we turn to annual data from the Pennsylvania Department of Internal Affairs[18] for factory employment and to population censuses for changes in the distribution of total employment at decennial intervals from 1910 to 1950.

When the industries of the city and the five-county area are classified into two broad groups of nondurable goods, chiefly consumers' goods, and of durable goods, chiefly producers' goods, those producing nondurable goods are found to have maintained employment levels between World Wars I and II to a much greater extent than the industries producing durable goods, here as elsewhere. For the period from 1919 to 1950, employment in textiles declined while that in apparel increased in both the city and the Pennsylvania counties[19] surrounding it. (Chart 1 and Appendix Table 5) The trend in food and tobacco products and in paper and printing was generally upward in the city and area between 1919 and 1950, while that in petroleum products was stationary in the city and slightly upward in its immediate environs. In all metal products, employment fluctuated more widely; it was high in both the city and its environs at the end of World Wars I and II but fell to very low levels in the thirties.

There are 22 subclasses of the major manufacturing industry groups that can be compared over the same period in which 5,000 or more workers were employed in Philadelphia either in 1923, 1939, or 1947. The trends in employment in these segments are of particular significance to the local economy. Table 3 presents data for these industries at intervals from 1919 to 1950.

Textile Products Industries

The long-term demand for labor in local textile industries is vul-

---

that the proportion of employment in these industries in plants located in the Philadelphia Metropolitan Area is also high relative to the structure of national employment.

18 These data have been converted to the classification used in the *1939 Census of Manufactures* and adjusted for unspecified items by reference to directories published by the Department. It may be noted that the data include reports from establishments with less than $5,000 value of product, that the series excludes employment in government productive establishments and salary workers, and may be subject to some downward bias in terms of coverage of new enterprises.

19 Bucks, Chester, Delaware, Montgomery.

CHART 1—Annual Average Number of Factory Wage Earners in Selected Industry Groups, Philadelphia and Philadelphia Five-County Area, 1919-1950

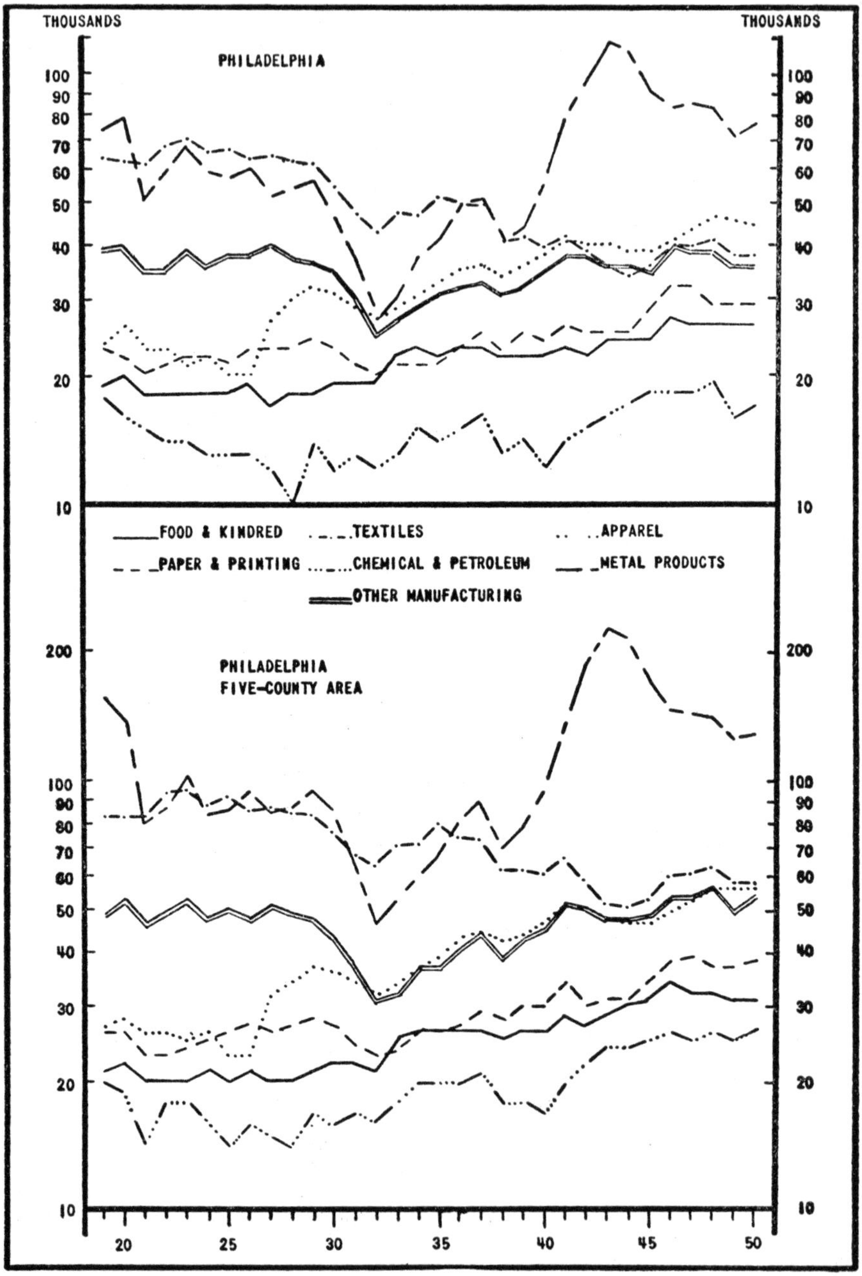

SOURCE: Appendix table 5

Table 3

AVERAGE ANNUAL EMPLOYMENT OF FACTORY WAGE EARNERS IN SELECTED MANUFACTURING INDUSTRIES[a]
AT SELECTED DATES, 1919-1950
PHILADELPHIA FIVE-COUNTY AREA

Industry	1919	1923	1929	1933	1937	1939	1943	1945	1947	1950
Textile Products										
Woolen and worsted goods and yarns	23,500	22,200	12,800	10,700	12,800	11,700	12,400	12,300	14,300	12,700
Carpets and rugs	5,800	8,400	5,000	3,900	3,200	4,200	2,000	2,300	4,600	4,400
Cotton goods	7,100	9,600	7,900	4,800	4,400	3,700	4,700	3,800	3,300	2,900
Silk and rayon goods	7,600	11,300	9,700	8,800	7,900	6,100	3,500	4,000	4,600	4,200
Hosiery	13,300	16,700	27,300	22,800	20,900	15,800	9,000	8,600	10,000	9,800
Dyeing and finishing	5,800	6,200	4,200	4,400	5,700	5,600	5,700	6,100	7,100	7,900
Metal Products										
Locomotives	16,000	6,900	4,400	900	3,600	2,800	13,100	11,100	7,200	4,000
Radios and parts	—	—	7,900	6,100	7,300	3,300	7,900	5,400	7,000	10,700
Industrial machinery	10,400	8,900	12,300	6,600	11,100	9,600	21,000	18,600	18,000	16,300
Automobiles	8,800	11,400	14,400	7,500	12,200	11,200	20,200[b]	18,000[b]	17,500[b]	15,200
Shipbuilding	58,000	9,500	2,600	1,600	4,200	5,800	46,800[c]	28,300[c]	4,100[c]	2,000
Electrical machinery, apparatus, and supplies	4,700	6,800	7,500	3,900	6,900	5,500	15,100	13,000	13,800	12,700
Apparel										
Men's clothing	6,600	7,100	16,800	16,200	19,800	19,100	20,500	20,100	23,400	22,300
Women's clothing	8,000	4,800	9,200	9,100	13,300	14,500	16,100	16,300	17,000	20,600
Other Products										
Bread and bakery products	5,000	7,300	8,000	8,000	8,900	8,600	8,600	9,100	9,700	9,500
Cigars	9,200	10,800	9,700	6,400	8,300	7,600	7,200	6,300	7,300	5,400
Paper and pulp	5,500	6,700	5,200	4,700	5,100	5,600	5,700	4,900	4,800	4,500
Job and newspaper printing	13,300	10,800	14,900	12,100	14,200	14,200	13,200	14,600	17,600	17,300
Gasoline	6,500	6,100	7,800	8,000	8,800	6,800	6,200	7,500	8,400	8,300
Leather tanning	5,900	5,000	4,900	4,600	4,400	3,900	3,100	2,800	3,300	3,200
Confectionery	4,100	4,000	3,300	3,600	3,800	4,100	4,100	4,500	5,400	5,300
Boxes—paper, cardboard, and fiber	3,300	3,400	3,200	3,600	4,200	4,300	5,200	7,200	7,800	8,500

Source: Pennsylvania Department of Internal Affairs (See Appendix Table 5).

[a] These subclasses employed 5,000 or more workers in 1923, 1939, or 1947. They exclude certain categories of iron and steel and other metal products for which comparable data for these dates could not be obtained.

[b] Differs from rounded figures shown in Appendix Table 5 because plants converted to production of aircraft during World War II are included here.

[c] Excludes employment at Philadelphia Naval Base and shipyards at Camden.

nerable to changes in consumption habits, changes in the location of the industries, the substitution of one type of fiber for another, and other technological changes that modify labor requirements. The local industries that have been most seriously affected by such influences are carpets and rugs, woolen and worsted goods, silk and rayon goods, the weaving of upholstery materials,[20] and hosiery. (Table3)

When the carpet and rug industry was localized in Philadelphia at the beginning of this century, the average American home was carpeted from wall to wall. In later years, a vogue for hardwood floors, or for linoleum and other floor coverings, made inroads on the total volume of carpet and rugs demanded. Increasing demand for broadloom as opposed to narrow-loom rugs rendered the equipment of some local mills obsolete and all were affected by the reduction in the over-all demand for labor in carpet and rug mills. New mills with new equipment located elsewhere, and increasing severe competition, partially affected by differentials in wage rates, led to declining employment in the industry in this area.[21]

Changes in consumption habits also led to a decline in the nation's demand for woolen and worsted goods and for knitted outerwear and underwear. The dispersion of plants from original centers of manufacture affected the competitive position of plants located in the older centers and local employment declined. For a period of time, expansion in the silk and rayon industries offset declines in the woolen and worsted industries, but some Philadelphia silk mills did not shift to the production of synthetic fibers and others went out of business in a severe competitive struggle as the industry expanded in other locations.

Upholstery materials produced by relatively skilled labor in the Philadelphia area, the original designing and producing center for the country, ran into a consumer demand for "high" styling at cheaper prices in place of higher-priced goods so well constructed that they would " last a lifetime." Philadelphia upholstery materials were copied in cheaper constructions that could be made on a volume basis by cotton mills. These mills, in which wage-scales were lower, were scattered throughout the country and secured an increasing

---

20 Included in the "cotton goods" classification in the table.

21 Gladys L. Palmer, *Union Tactics and Economic Change* (Philadelphia: University of Pennsylvania Press, 1932), pp. 5-10.

share of the business that had formerly come to Philadelphia mills.[22]

An increase in the demand for full-fashioned hosiery accompanied a style of short skirts and led to rapid expansion of the local industry from 1919 to 1929. Differentials in labor costs between union and nonunion centers and expansion to secure higher profits led to dispersion of the industry in the late twenties. Subsequent style changes favoring sheer hose, which could be manufactured only on the newest equipment, gave a differential advantage to newer plants scattered throughout Pennsylvania and the southern states. The older Philadelphia mills, with a high proportion of obsolete equipment, were thereby placed at a competitive disadvantage, even when labor cost differentials were minimized as the result of union negotiations. During and after World War II, technological improvements in machine equipment entirely eliminated one occupation and reduced the labor requirements in others. All of these changes resulted in declines from the peak levels of local employment in 1929. The introduction of the more durable nylon in place of silk and rayon fibers reduced the over-all demand for labor in full-fashioned hoisery mills and increasing competitive pressures after World War II led to further declines in local employment. By the end of 1954, the only operations left in Philadelphia were dyeing and finishing processes employing about a thousand workers.[23]

Some Philadelphia textile mills adjusted to changes in consumer demand and replaced old equipment with new or, less frequently, supplemented one type of product with another. Nevertheless, many firms went out of business and were not replaced by new units. A few branch plants of Philadelphia concerns were established elsewhere in the hope of securing some differential in costs. All of the industries discussed here are characterized by relatively high labor costs, and regional differentials in such costs, which were much higher fifteen or twenty years ago than they are today, undoubtedly played a part in these developments. Equally important, however, was the character of the changes in consumption habits or in technology that rendered obsolete some of the machine equipment in the industry

22 C. C. Balderston, *et. al.*, *The Philadelphia Upholstery Weaving Industry* (Philadelphia: University of Pennsylvania Press, 1932), pp. 157-61.

23 "City Hosiery Mill to Close: Last Full-fashioned Plant," *The Evening Bulletin* (Philadelphia), December 16, 1954.

and the skills of some of its labor supply, regardless of differentials in labor costs.

A question undoubtedly occurs to the reader as to whether Philadelphia textile labor priced itself out of the market during these developments. The first point in this connection is that dispersion of the industry to new centers occurred in both unionized and non-unionized branches of the textile industry. Viewed in historical perspective, there is some evidence that a few textile unions might have salvaged more employment for their members by a more judicious timing of their willingness to accept the savings in labor costs that were eventually negotiated, either through wage reductions or other economies, but the evidence is by no means conclusive.[24] One local union in the carpet industry refused to make any concessions when local plants were threatened by outside competion and eventually went out of existence after a prolonged strike.[25] The chances are that industrial statesmanship on the part of both management and labor on specific occasions might have achieved a more orderly retreat. In the hosiery industry, on the other hand, where both technological changes and shifts in the location of the industry affected employment in Philadelphia (and other old centers), union policy was for a long period directed towards increasing the efficiency of union members and maintaining the competitive position of union plants within the framework of collective bargaining relations.[26] But even so, the industry was lost to this area.

It is possible that in an industry subject to great fluctuations in profits, such as textiles, the age of an enterprise leads to managerial lethargy, or that, over time, enterprisers decide to limit or spread their risks by investing in different types of enterprise or by locating in new as well as in old centers. Whatever the cause, recent capital investment in local textile industries has taken the form of new machines or modifications in equipment rather than new plants. New textile plants appear to be springing up in most instances in southern

24 Palmer, *op. cit.*, chaps. IV and V.

25 *Ibid.*, chap. III.

26 George W. Taylor, "Hosiery," chap. 9 in *How Collective Bargaining Works*, edited by Harry A. Millis (New York: Twentieth Century Fund, 1942); Thomas Kennedy, *Effective Labor Arbitration* (Philadelphia: University of Pennsylvania Press, 1948), chap. VIII. See also award of the Wage Tribunal of the Full-Fashioned Hosiery Manufacturers of America, Inc. and American Federation of Hosiery Workers, March 3, 1950 (mimeographed).

locations. There is no indication in current developments of a reversal of the longer-term influences that have resulted in unstable or declining employment in the specialized textile industries that were once the most important single employer of labor in Philadelphia.

Metal Products Industries

The metal-working industries of Philadelphia were also affected by changes in the geographic location of plants, in technology, and indirectly in consumption habits. In addition, because of the potential uses of their equipment for the production of munitions they have experienced periods of very rapid expansion and contraction. (Table 3)

Trends in employment in the manufacture of transportation equipment between World Wars I and II were mixed but generally downward. Shipbuilding employment reached a high peak in World War I, but declined drastically after the close of the war and was later affected by the naval disarmament program and the loss of national shipping business to foreign carriers. Much the same pattern was repeated during and after World War II. Although the manufacture of railroad and streetcar equipment continued at high levels for several years after World War I, employment in this industry was affected by a severe decline in demand during the depression, by changes in labor requirements as the result of the introduction of new types of equipment, and by competition from other centers of manufacture. In the automotive industry, the manufacture of automobile bodies and trucks developed locally during this period, but the major expansion of the industry and its subsidiary activities occurred in the Midwest. The rapid growth of the automobile industry in and around Detroit led to expansion of brass foundry work as well as to the growth of plants making machine-tool products and automobile parts in that area. These developments had adverse effects on local employment in various types of metal products. Early expansion of the aircraft-engine industry also bypassed the Philadelphia area for the most part, although during both wars there was employment in aircraft production as a result of conversion of other facilities or the development of new enterprises. Since World War II, however, the production of helicopters has had a favorable start in this area.

In the manufacture of industrial machinery and electrical machinery and supplies, on the other hand, local trends in employment followed national trends. The latter industry received a major impetus as a result of experience in World War I and later expansion of the demand for radios and electrical equipment and supplies. The location of the electrical machinery industry here may seem to be at variance with a general westward trend in location of this industry, but is probably accounted for in terms of the advantages of an early start by several large units and nearness to engineering laboratories, other manufacturing units, and an important segment of the market, as well as to a skilled labor supply with experience in metal-working occupations. Since World War II, the production of television and electronic equipment has expanded rapidly.

At an early stage of its history, Philadelphia was a major center of the iron and steel industries, but these industries moved west prior to World War I in order to secure advantages in the costs of fuel and raw materials. Heavy demand for iron and steel products during World War I temporarily interrupted a downward trend in local employment in this industry. Although there have been a few general and specialized iron and steel plants in the area, most of the expansion of the industry between World Wars I and II occurred in the Great Lakes region. Currently, this westward movement is being reversed. The near exhaustion of the iron ore resources in the Lake Superior region during World War II led to greater dependence on imports, and Atlantic Seaboard communities now offer locational advantages to the iron and steel industries.[27] The "basing-point" decision on freight rates has also modified the relative locational advantages for metal fabricating plants. One large basic steel works has recently located in the area and it is anticipated that other steel works and new metal fabricating plants will eventually be located here unless the building of the St. Lawrence Seaway, which will facilitate transportation of Labrador iron ore to the Midwest, again modifies this pattern of locational advantage.

---

27 Walter Isard forecasts a firm economic position for the eastern part of the Middle Atlantic States as a result of this trend. He estimates that the location of the steel industry in the Delaware River Valley will give rise to 170,000 new jobs during the next decade.—"The Economic Consequences of the Changing Geography of American Industry," *Proceedings of the Sixth Annual Meeting of the Industrial Relations Research Association* (Washington, December 1953).

Other Industries

Nation-wide changes in consumption habits have also influenced recent developments in other local industries. Increased use of the automobile led to the expansion of oil refining and the refineries located in the Philadelphia area followed national trends in expanding employment. (Table 3) This is the largest refining area on the Atlantic Seaboard and local port traffic is dominated by this industry.

General changes in consumption habits and modes of living led to increases in employment in food processing throughout the country, and this area was no exception. For example, local employment in the manufacture of bread and bakery products, ice cream, and, after the repeal of Prohibition, of malt liquors showed moderate increases, although the number of wage jobs fluctuated in other food products and declined in sugar refining. Increases in employment in the paper industry, particularly in the production of paper boxes and fiber containers, accompanied the development of new methods of packaging goods for sale. Employment in the manufacture of cigars and in leather tanning, on the other hand, declined.[28] Local employment was adversely affected by nation-wide changes in the demand for cigars and for the type of leather goods produced here, and, in the case of the former, by technological changes that modified labor requirements in the industry.

In other manufacturing industries where employment of wage earners gained during the years under review, a variety of influences appears to have been significant. Important industries in this group were men's clothing, women's apparel, and printing and publishing. All three were well established in the area prior to World War I and all are characterized by high or moderately high labor costs. Local plants in all three industries cater to a market of moderate or low prices. There is reason to believe that local expansion of employment in these industries, especially during a depression, was occasionally at the expense of employment in other centers, since in a depression, moderate-priced goods are in great demand and low-cost manufacturing centers usually gain at the expense of centers

28 In the summer of 1954, one of the city's oldest tanning companies closed its plant and laid off 500 workers. The reason given for this layoff was excess capacity for processing a declining supply of imported skins.—*The Evening Bulletin* (Philadelphia), June 17, 1954.

producing higher-priced goods at higher costs. Local gains in printing and publishing may have been at the expense of New York City, and expansion of production in men's clothing is known to have had adverse effects on the Chicago and Rochester clothing markets. That these gains were not temporary, however, is substantiated by trends after 1939. The apparel industry and substantial segments of the printing industry are unionized. Later unionization of the Philadelphia apparel industry, as compared with other centers, may have given this area more competitive advantages prior to 1930. Since that time, local union leadership has developed long-term policies directed toward increasing the union's membership and, at the same time, maintaining or improving the competitive position of the local industries.

Changes in the Industrial Distribution of Total Employment

A broader perspective on changes in the economic structure of Philadelphia is gained by a comparison of the ways in which the workers in the city and in the nation made a living in 1910 and 1950. Between these two dates, dramatic changes took place in the national economy; and in general, fewer workers were required to produce a higher standard of living at the later date. In 1910, for each 10,000 persons in the nation's population, it took 3,856 workers to produce a gross national product of $556 per capita (in 1929 dollars). In 1950, on the other hand, only 3,732 workers were needed for an output of $1,229 per capita (in 1929 dollars). This increase in productivity occurred at the same time that average hours of work declined from about 58 to 42 per week.[29]

During this span of four decades, new factory products and means of transportation and communication were substituted for old. Many activities that had formerly been performed in homes were transferred to commercial establishments, as in the case of food preparation and laundry and dry-cleaning establishments. There was an increase in the employment of nurses, dentists, and other profes-

---

29 Gladys L. Palmer and Ann R. Miller, "The Occupational and Industrial Distribution of Employment, 1910-1950," chap. VI in *Manpower in the United States: Problems and Policies*, edited by William Haber *et al.* for the Industrial Relations Research Association (New York: Harper & Brothers, 1954), pp. 83, 85.

sional persons and certain types of service workers, an increase that reflected the effects of a general rise in the standard of living as well as of increased specialization of activities. Some part of a decline of employment relative to population in manufacturing, construction, and transportation resulted from technological changes that modified the labor requirements in these industries. A decline in the extractive industries accompanied the urbanization of the population, the increasing productivity in the extractive industries, and to some extent, the exhaustion of resources.

Technical Appendix Table A presents estimates of employment by industry for residents of Philadelphia and nonfarm workers in the United States in 1910, in terms of the major classifications used in 1950.[30] Parallel data are not available to make this comparison for the Standard Metropolitan Area of Philadelphia. These estimates refer to residents of Philadelphia rather than to employees of plants located in Philadelphia. They include self-employed persons, managers and owners, government employees, and a small group of unpaid family workers, as well as private wage and salary workers. The trends in total employment, however, are weighted by the experience of private wage and salary workers, who constituted 81 per cent of the total employed in 1950.[31]

For all Philadelphia residents, as distinct from wage-workers employed in plants located within the city limits, the greatest increases in manufacturing over the three decades occurred in chemicals and petroleum, food products, and paper products. The greatest declines occurred in textiles, leather and leather goods, lumber products and

---

30 See Technical Appendix for methods of deriving the 1910 estimates.

31 In addition, there are other sources of difference between employment as reported by establishments and by the population in a census or sample survey. All persons on payrolls are reported in an establishment series and there may be duplication because of turnover and dual job-holding. In a population survey, each person is accounted for but once and if he holds more than one job in a given period is usually classified on the job from which he receives most income or works the longest hours. An establishment series, on the one hand, reports jobs filled in plants located in a given area, while on the other hand, a population survey reports the economic activities of the residents of a given area. Since there was less commutation across county or city limits in 1910 than in 1950, the differences between data from establishment and population reports have increased over time. A final point may also be noted. In the manufacturing employment data cited in the preceding section, no reports were received from Government productive establishments, such as navy yards and arsenals. In the data from the Census of Population used here, Philadelphia residents employed by such agencies are classified in manufacturing.

furniture, and tobacco. The metal and machinery industries and the printing and apparel industries showed modest increases when measured from 1910 levels, and a heterogeneous group of "miscellaneous" manufacturing industries showed a substantial decline. If one disregards the experience in World Wars I and II and views the longer term of years from 1910 to 1950, the employment of workers residing in Philadelphia who were attached to the metal products industries showed great improvement despite postwar declines in the demand for labor in certain segments of the industries located in the city and its Pennsylvania environs.

In nonmanufacturing industries, the greatest increases in total employment between 1910 and 1950 occurred in business and repair services,[32] finance, insurance and real estate, public administration,[33] and professional services. (Technical Appendix Table A) Although the greatest declines occurred in the extractive industries and personal services, there was also a decline in transportation and construction.

It is unfortunate that data are not available for all the intervening years in these decades to measure more exactly the kind of transfers or other employment changes that took place in the entire local economy before and after World War I. The displacement of some Philadelphia workers from factory jobs after the war was obviously offset by increases in employment in nonmanufacturing industries between 1920 and 1930. Employment in the industries most comparable to manufacturing in the types of skills required, however, particularly construction and transportation, remained almost stationary from 1920 to 1930 and, by 1940, employment levels in these industries were substantially below those of 1910. The major industries that expanded throughout most or all of the entire period under consideration were primarily those employing a relatively high pro-

---

32 In the case of business and repair services, some of this increase may be fictitious, since it was difficult to make the conversion to this classification for 1910 data.

33 Employment in public administration refers to employment in the Mint, the Postal Service, local police and fire departments, national defense, and offices of administrative agencies in federal, state, and local governments. Employment in productive establishments operated by the Federal Government, such as arsenals and navy yards, is classified under manufacturing; employment in schools and hospitals is classified under professional service.

portion of clerical and professional persons rather than skilled craftsmen, semiskilled operatives, or laborers.

The broader perspective on industrial trends for Philadelphia workers that disregards the temporary effects of World Wars I and II, takes account of increased commutation across city lines, and covers all groups in the city's labor force, modifies some of the findings of the preceding section. As might be expected, it can now be seen that the declines in manufacturing employment from 1910 levels were not so drastic as from the greatly expanded levels of World War I. Despite shifts in the character of the metal products industries and their location in relation to the city's limits, employment of the city's residents in these industries showed a substantial increase.[34] The decline in textile employment from 1910 levels, however, was substantial. Gross declines from 1910 levels were relatively more important in manufacturing employment than in nonmanufacturing industries.

Table 4

GROSS CHANGES IN EMPLOYMENT BY INDUSTRY GROUP
PHILADELPHIA, 1910-1950

(Industries ranked by relative importance in 1910 within manufacturing and nonmanufacturing groups)
(in thousands)

Manufacturing	+26	Nonmanufacturing	+118
Metal industries, etc.	+34	Trade	+ 53
Textile mill products	–25	Personal services	– 32
Apparel and accessories	+ 7	Transportation	– 3
Other manufactures	–16	Communications and utilities	+ 10
Printing and publishing	+ 4	Construction	+ 1
Food and kindred products	+13	Professional and related services	+ 33
Leather and leather products	– 4	Public administration	+ 24
Chemicals and petroleum	+11	Finance, insurance	+ 19
Lumber and furniture	– 2	Extractive industries	– 5
Paper and paper products	+ 4	Business and repair services	+ 16
Tobacco manufactures	– *	Entertainment	+ 2

Gross increase	+231
Gross decline	– 87
Net change	+144

Source: Technical Appendix Table A.
* Less than 500.

[34] The data on employment in metal-products industries cited in the preceding section do not include plants located in the Camden Industrial Area in which some Philadelphia residents are employed.

The major loss in the latter industries was attributable to declines in employment in the personal service industries, chiefly domestic service.

These shifts in the ways in which Philadelphians have made their living take on more significance if account is taken of changes in the size of the city's population. (Charts 2 and 3, Appendix Table 6) Total employment relative to population in Philadelphia in 1950 was about 10 per cent below 1910 levels. Although the most substantial declines occurred in the extractive industries, personal services, and transportation and construction, manufacturing employment in 1950 was 18 per cent below 1910 levels. Within manufacturing, the most important decline was in the textile industries. For the most part, local trends in employment relative to population followed national trends in nonagricultural employment relative to nonfarm population although the magnitude of the changes differed. One exception occurred in the case of printing and publishing, which increased in the nation but declined in Philadelphia. (Appendix Table 6) The only industries in which the city's rate of increase outpaced that of the nation during this period were the manufacture of food products, finance and insurance, business and repair services, and professional and related services. For each 10,000 persons in the populations compared, the rate of decline was lower for Philadelphia than for the United States in the manufacture of apparel and tobacco products and in transportation. These industries have maintained or improved their competitive position as measured by national employment trends.

The trends in employment, just discussed, naturally resulted in changes in the structure of local employment during this period. There was an increase in the relative importance of nonmanufacturing compared with manufacturing industries and the ranking of specific industries also changed. These changes were more spectacular in the case of women than of men. (Appendix Table 7) Although most changes in the distribution of employment in Philadelphia between 1910 and 1950 were paralleled in the nation, a decline in the relative importance of local employment in the textile industries was especially marked. For example, textile manufactures occupied second rank as an employer of women in Philadelphia in 1910, but had dropped to sixth place by 1950. Again, in the employment of

CHART 2—Percentage Change in Employment in Manufacturing Industries Relative to Population, Philadelphia and the United States, 1910-1950

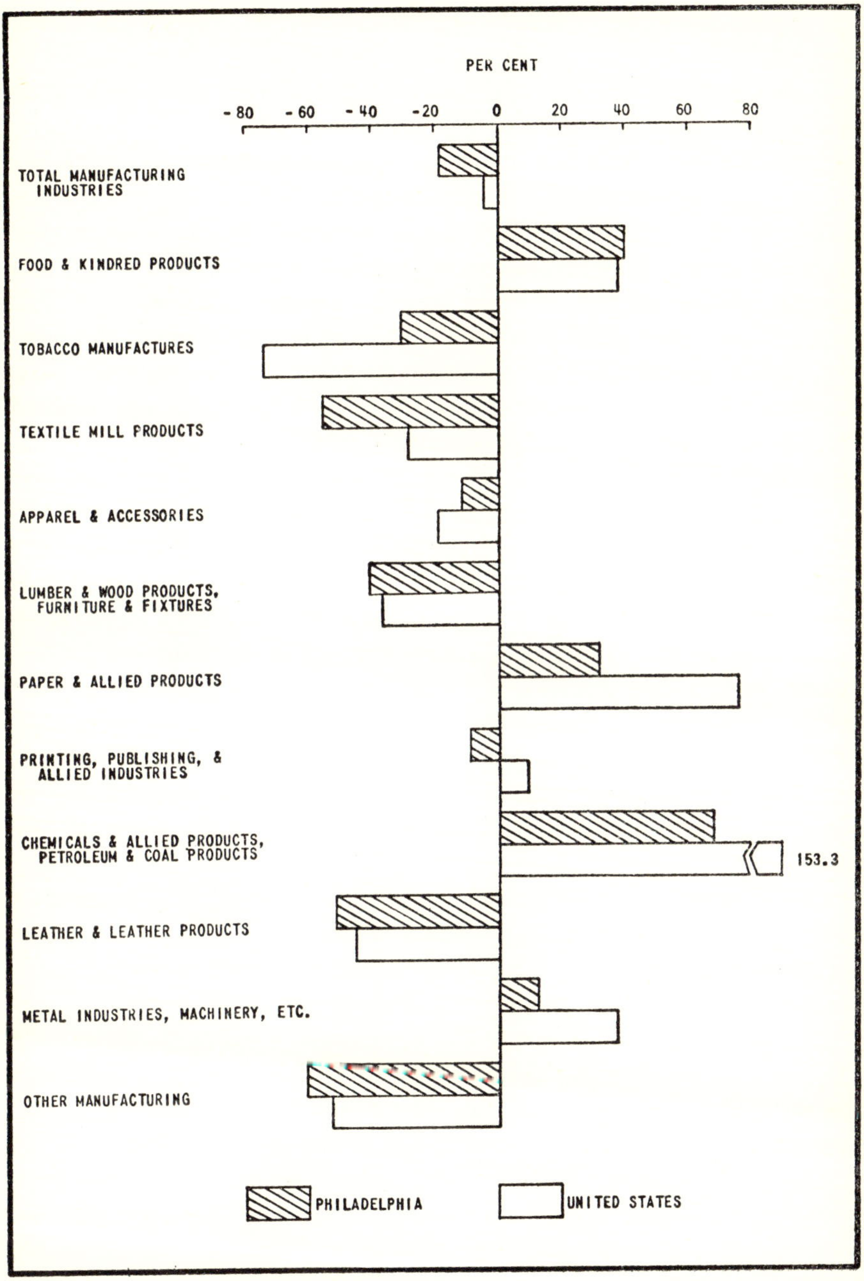

SOURCE: Appendix table 6

CHART 3—Percentage Change in Employment in Nonmanufacturing Industries Relative to Population, Philadelphia and the United States, 1910-1950

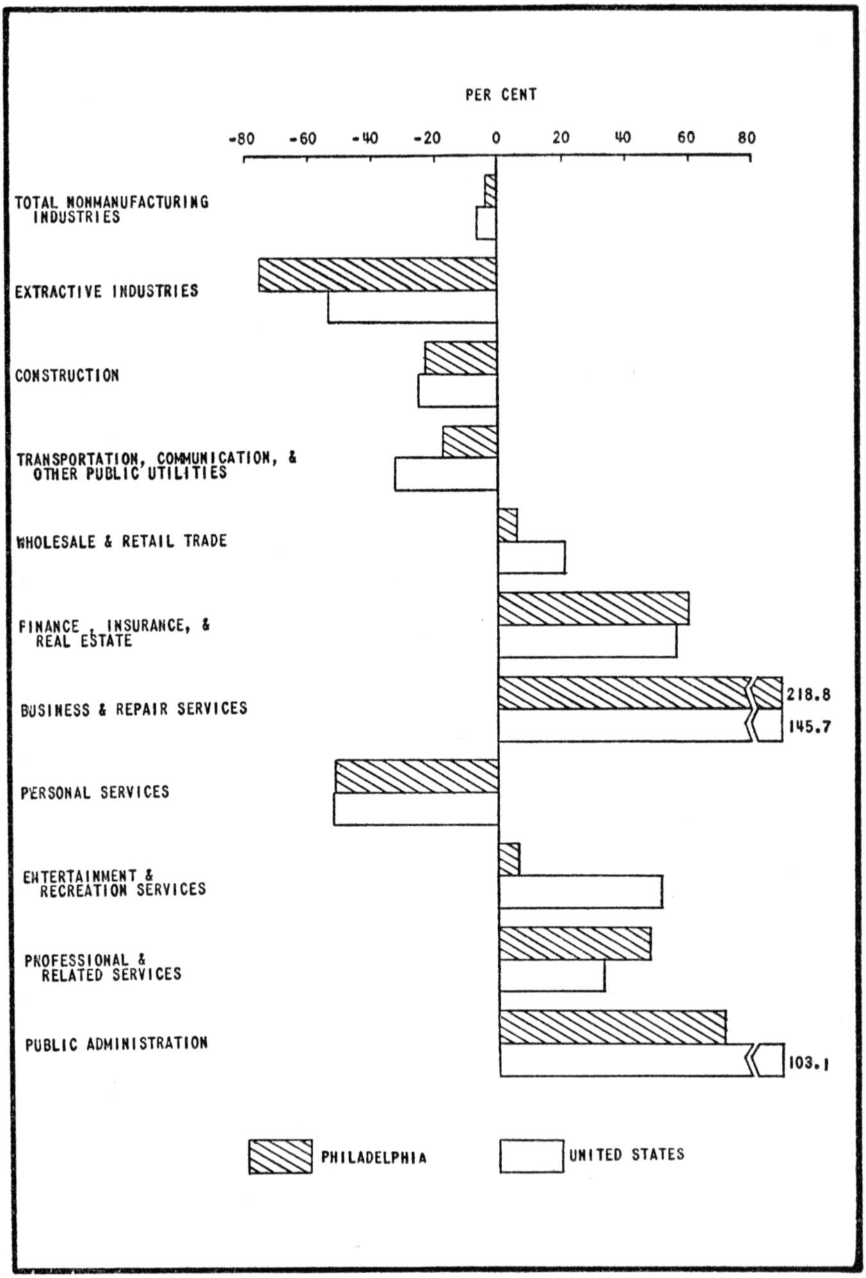

SOURCE: Appendix table 6

women, personal service industries dropped from first to second place, trade rose from third to first place, and the professional services rose from fifth to third place in rank between 1910 and 1950. For Philadelphia workers of both sexes, trade remained in first place at both dates, metal manufacturing rose from third to second place, personal services dropped from second to fifth in rank, and the transportation group moved from fourth up to third place. These structural changes brought the distribution of total employment in the city closer to that of the nation.

Despite a decline in the relative importance of manufacturing employment in recent decades, Philadelphia's factories still perform a basic function in the nation's workshops. In 1950 there were 11 major manufacturing industry groups in which the proportion of total employment in the city was greater than the corresponding proportion of national employment, whereas there was only one such major group in nonmanufacturing. (Appendix Table 8) As noted earlier, the number of minor subdivisions of manufacturing in which the city has offered locational advantages is more than double this figure. This concentration of manufacturing is more pronounced for the Philadelphia Standard Metropolitan Area than for the city and holds whether employment is measured in terms of persons residing in the area or of plants located there.

Implications of Shifts in the Economic Functions of Philadelphia

The years between World Wars I and II marked an important stage in the economic development of Philadelphia and its environs as well as of the nation. Major economic changes in the manufacturing economy that had been interrupted by World War I came to a focus in the two decades that followed it. The most important changes (for Philadelphia) were the steady westward march of the nation's durable goods industries and the dispersion of the textile industries from older centers, as well as shifts in the demand for certain other goods produced in the area. The net effect of these broad changes in the national economy was to redistribute the demand for factory labor, creating some competitive disadvantages for older centers like Philadelphia. Superimposed on these developments were technological changes that reduced or modified the labor requirements in manufacturing generally. Despite diversification of the city's products, one stage or another of processing various items was affected by some or all of these developments. Most local trends in employment paralleled those in the nation, but some declines were more severe locally than nationally. A few local industries showed higher rates of growth than their counterparts in the nation, but they tend to employ relatively few persons. From the point of view of their importance to the local economy in earlier decades, employment declines in textile products and personal services were the most significant.

Although the depression of the thirties reduced the total demand for labor to low points everywhere, many other areas recovered more rapidly or more completely than Philadelphia. In this respect, the city was affected by the maladjustments created by longer-term changes and by the slow rate of recovery in the region of which it is a major center. Indirectly, its prosperity was affected by the economic misfortunes of some of the major industries in that region, such as anthracite mining. Despite shifts in relative importance or in levels of employment that have been noted, manufacturing continues to be highly significant to the city's economic base and a manifestly large number of diversified types of manufacturing have found locational advantages here.

Like Milwaukee and Cincinnati, Philadelphia has many manufacturing enterprises that are family owned and operated. Local plants tend to be small or moderate in size, even in industries that are typically large scale. There is notably little employment in the branch plants of large national corporations or in integrated, large-scale business units. Since most local factories produce a limited range of products and many enterprises are extremely specialized in equipment, their investment risks may be limited, but the economic risks of the operations are greater. In terms of size, Philadelphia plants are like those of St. Louis. In terms of the character of its products, Philadelphia probably resembles Newark, although textiles are relatively more important in Philadelphia and the heavy metal industries in Newark.

The area's growth and industrial characteristics, like those of most cities, are partly the result of its basic economic advantages and partly the result of the initiative and leadership of the business community.

Historical accident has also played a role. The advantages of an early start under favorable conditions led to concentrations of the textile and metal-working industries in this area. Thrifty German, Scotch, and English businessmen laid the foundations of many a family business and fortune in these industries. The Quakers of past decades were largely responsible for the development of Philadelphia's "quality" products that were sold under trademarks of national repute. Philadelphia business, like the community of which it is a part, has been considered conservative in its outlook and it is probable that traditional ways of doing business have outlasted their usefulness on occasion. Nevertheless, it is no mean accomplishment to remain in business "at the same stand" for 50 or 100 years, and the advantages to a community of stability of business enterprise that is primarily of local origin should not be minimized.

There is no evidence that the size of local plants and their form of organization have had any direct effect on the fortunes of local industries, although they may have had indirect influences. The predominant characteristics of local enterprises differ from the prevailing trends in national business organization and these differences may enhance other competitive difficulties in an older center. On the other hand, the relative staying-power of many local business enterprises in a wide variety of industries argues that competitive disadvantages have been successfully met despite these attributes.

It is ironical that a city where Quakers have played such an important economic role should owe so much of its development to wars. From the time of the American Revolution to the present, local shipbuilding and the production of munitions have made essential contributions to the national economy. They have been carried on in peacetime as well as in war, but in war periods, the expansion of the facilities existing in this area provided a quick way to secure large-scale production. Atomic warfare may alter the advantages of seaboard communities and the character of munitions production in the future, but fortunately for this area, its "swords" can be turned into "ploughshares."

Wars have brought rapid expansion to the Philadelphia area but they have usually been followed by substantial declines in employment. Some gains followed the starts made in a particular industry as the result of war orders, but peacetime expansion in this area after

World War I did not reach the rate of expansion in the country as a whole or of that in some other cities. Wars tend to distort the structure of the national economy and this tendency is even more marked in a war-industry center like Philadelphia. Reconversion to peacetime pursuits leaves segments of capital equipment and facilities idle and requires extensive shifts on the part of workers to find new avenues of gainful employment in the same or other areas. The changes in Philadelphia's population and labor force that accompanied the changes in the structure of the local economy outlined in this chapter constitute the subject matter of Chapters IV and V. The effects of war and reconversion to peacetime pursuits are discussed in more detail with respect to the experience in World War II and postwar years in Chapter VI.

Chapter IV

Labor-Force Changes in Recent Decades

PHILADELPHIA has always been noted as a skilled labor center and therefore has attracted workers with specialized skills from Europe and other parts of this country. This was particularly the case for the textile and metal products industries that had had an early start in the city and its environs. For many decades, there was a tradition among the city's workers that young people must learn a "trade," in the sense of becoming proficient in a skilled craft or a relatively skilled machine-operating job. Young workers frequently followed the occupation of their parents, and many families had more than one worker and more than one generation of workers employed in the same industry or plant. Workers' knowledge of materials and processes and of some of management's problems in an industry was a concomitant development of the influence of family and community environment on occupational choice, of the small size and nature of ownership of most plants, and of a traditional spirit of craftsmanship that characterized the city's labor force.

Until World War I, workers tended to live within walking or easy commuting distance of factories and this accounted for concentrations of workers' homes near specific kinds of plants in various sections of the city. The northeast, for example, became a textile center, central city, an apparel manufacturing center, and the northern section, a metal products center. Although dispersion from the center of both population and industry has modified this pattern, some concentration of plants and of workers' homes in the vicinity is characteristic of the city today.

Population and employment were expanding in the two decades prior to 1920. Rapid growth of the textile and metal products industries was accompanied by a considerable foreign immigration. Because production requirements during World War I were met by the conversion and expansion of existing facilities and equipment and by the building of new war plants in established manufacturing centers, Philadelphia and its environs gained in population and its employment levels were high. In the decade from 1920 to 1930, however, the population of the city grew at a much less rapid rate; it declined slightly between 1930 and 1940, and expanded again between 1940 and 1950.

Concomitant with this growth of the population there were changes in its age, sex, and racial and nationality composition that affected the size and characteristics of the labor force. Industrial changes also occurred that led to shifts in the demand for workers with given types of skills. Although many of the changes in the economy of Philadelphia during these decades paralleled national developments, the impact of some was more severe locally than nationally. Before discussing these trends in greater detail, it should be noted that most of the data used in this analysis of the labor force refer to experience in the city of Philadelphia rather than in the broader industrial area of which it is the nucleus. This emphasis is unavoidable because data are not available for the entire period to describe the experience of the area.

Widening of the Labor-Market Area

It was the practice of Philadelphia personnel managers during World War I to recruit workers from within a radius of three miles of a plant. This practice, representing a "rule of thumb" measure of areas beyond which recruiting brought excessive turnover or absenteeism of workers, probably reflected the limits of typical commuting distances at that time. Since workers tended to live in the neighborhood where plants were located, the area was, in essence, composed of a series of neighborhood labor markets.

Following World War I, some plants moved from the city to suburban locations, initiating a trend that has increased in recent years. In addition, many residents of the city moved to the suburbs, as improved roads and public transportation facilities and increased use of the automobile widened the geographic area over which it was possible to commute. Some concentration of plant and worker locations nevertheless continue in the city.

It is doubtful that there was much commuting across city limits in 1910, except between Camden and Philadelphia. By 1950, however, commuting between the counties of Pennsylvania, New Jersey, and Delaware that border on the Delaware River Basin was an established practice. Many Philadelphia residents now work outside the city limits, and many residents of nearby communities are employed in business enterprises located in the city. No adequate measures of the increase in such commuting are available, but it is estimated that in 1940 approximately 25,000 Philadelphia residents, chiefly industrial workers, were employed outside the city, and 40,000 persons, chiefly "white-collar" workers, commuted into the city to work.[1] During World War II, the net balance was out of the city, with an estimated employment of 65,000 Philadelphia residents in the city's environs.[2] By this time, the most populous sections of the eight counties comprising the Standard Metropolitan Area were, in effect, a single labor market.

Population Changes from 1900 to 1950

In the decades prior to 1900 the city of Philadelphia had gained population at a faster rate than the surrounding area. Between 1900 and 1920, the city's rate of gain declined and the area's remained stable in terms of earlier decades. Subsequent to 1920, the rate of growth in both the city and the area declined further, but by 1940 the city had lost population and the area had gained only two per cent over the preceding decade. In 1950 the area increased at a considerably higher rate than the city. These developments were associated with significant changes in the composition of the population.

Increases in the size of the city's population up to 1920, were associated with substantial increases in foreign-born population and migration from other areas. (Appendix Table 9) After World War

1 Gladys L. Palmer, *War Labor Supply Problems in Philadelphia and Its Environs,* Research Report No. 5 (Philadelphia: Industrial Research Department, University of Pennsylvania, 1942), p. 37.

2 Gladys L. Palmer, *The Philadelphia Labor Market in 1944,* Research Report No. 8 (Philadelphia: Industrial Research Department, University of Pennsylvania, 1944), p. 13.

I, immigration from foreign countries declined, although persons continued to move to the city from other parts of the country, particularly Negroes from the southern states. Between 1920 and 1940, the direction of movement was reversed. Some Philadelphia residents moved to the surrounding counties to live, and others left the area. It is estimated that at least 100,000 persons left the city in each of these decades.[3] This out-migration was offset by in-migration and high birth rates in the twenties, but in the thirties low birth rates and less in-migration resulted in the net loss mentioned above. The foreign-born population declined even further by 1950, falling below that of 1900, even though the city's population increased. All of these developments had the net effect of increasing the proportion of the population in older age groups, of reducing the ratio of males to females, of lowering the proportion of foreign-born to total population, and of increasing the proportion of nonwhite to total population. This pattern of change was characteristic of both the city and the area, although it was more marked in the case of the city.

Changes in the Size and Composition of the Labor Force

Despite certain changes in the size and composition of the population which would have had the effect of decreasing the size of the city's labor force, it increased from 1900 to 1930, declined slightly in 1940, and rose above 1930 levels in 1950. More specifically, the male labor force increased up to 1930 and declined after that date, while the female labor force continued to increase throughout this period. (Appendix Table 10) A persistent increase in the female labor force is associated with increases in the sex ratio of the population, with shorter hours of work, and with developing opportunities for the employment of women in "white-collar" occupations and "light" factory work. In addition to some loss to the city's labor force through out-migration, the decline in the male labor force is associated with declining rates of labor-force participation as a result of the postponement of entrance to the labor market because of

---

[3] Data prior to 1950 in this section are summarized from Simon S. Kuznets, *The Population of Philadelphia and Environs,* Part I of a report to the Philadelphia City Planning Commission (Philadelphia: Institute of Local and State Government, University of Pennsylvania, 1946).

longer schooling for boys, and the earlier and increased retirement of older men.

In the case of women, similar considerations have affected the proportion of the youngest and oldest workers in the population. In the intermediate age groups, which have the largest numbers, other considerations must be taken into account. A decline in the female rate of labor-force participation from 1910 to 1920 (Table 5) may be associated with high marriage and birth rates during and immediately after World War I, and possibly with the decline in handicrafts, such as dressmaking, that employed relatively large numbers of women in earlier decades. After 1920, increased participation by women 25 to 44 years of age more than offset declines in the employment of girls under 25 or of women over 64 years of age. The participation of the intermediate age groups of women is influenced by marriage and birth rates as they affect home responsibilities, by economic conditions as they affect family income, as well as by the expansion or decline of opportunities for the employment of women. The net effect of all of these developments was to increase the proportion of women in the city's labor force from 26 per cent in 1900 to 32 per cent in 1950.

These trends in labor-force participation since the turn of the century are not peculiar to the city, but reflect declining rates of participation for men and increasing rates for women in the nation.[4] (Table 5) It may be noted that the proportion of the population in the labor force has always been higher in Philadelphia than in the United States, and also higher in the city than in its environs, but these differences are narrowing and have not affected the trends over time.

Changes in the racial and nationality composition of the population have affected the composition of the labor force also. The nonwhite population of the city was only 5.5 per cent of the total in 1910 but increased to 18.3 per cent by 1950. The proportion of non-

---

[4] John D. Durand, *The Labor Force in the United States, 1890-1960* (New York: Social Science Research Council, 1948), chap. 2. In his analysis of labor-force changes, Durand omits the data for 1910 because they are out of line with trends in labor-force participation by age and sex from 1890 to 1940. What appears to be a decline in participation rates from 1910 to 1920 may therefore reflect a bias in the 1910 Census enumeration or unusually high levels of participation rates in 1910.

Table 5

PERCENTAGE OF POPULATION 14 YEARS OF AGE AND OVER IN THE LABOR FORCE, 1910-1950
Philadelphia, Philadelphia Standard Metropolitan Area, and the United States

Year	Philadelphia			Philadelphia Standard Metropolitan Area			United States		
	Total	Men	Women	Total	Men	Women	Total	Men	Women
1910	61.4	90.6	33.7	n.a.	n.a.	n.a.	57.9	88.4	25.2
1920	60.6	89.8	31.7	n.a.	n.a.	n.a.	55.6	86.4	23.3
1930	59.4	86.6	32.8	57.6	86.0	29.8	53.2	82.1	23.6
1940	56.7	81.2	33.8	55.4	80.6	31.4	52.7	79.7	25.7
1950	54.7	77.4	33.9	54.4	78.7	31.6	53.4	78.9	29.0

Source: Appendix Table 10.

white (mostly Negro) workers in the labor force rose from 7.5 per cent in 1910 to 17.6 per cent in 1950. During the same period, the proportion of foreign-born population in the city dropped from 24.8 to 11.2 per cent.

There are no statistical data on the nationality of foreign-born workers in the Philadelphia labor force during these years. Data on the nationality composition of the population, however, are available, (Appendix Table 9) and, since most foreign-born persons were of working age when they came to this country, their characteristics may be presumed to apply to those who entered the labor market. In 1900, almost a half of the foreign-born population of the city had come from Northern Europe, predominantly from the British Isles, but by 1950 this group represented slightly less than a fifth of the total. The proportions from Central Europe represented a fourth of the foreign-born population in 1950 and slightly more than a fourth in earlier decades. The greatest relative increase in the foreign-born population occurred in the group from Eastern and Southern Europe who constituted only 16 per cent of the foreign-born population in 1900, and 48 per cent in 1950. Russians (including Lithuanians) and Italians constituted the largest single groups from this part of Europe. In 1950, the largest single nationality groups of foreign birth were Russians and Lithuanians, Italians, Irishmen, Poles, and Germans.

Russian Jews and Italians and their descendants are employed in substantial numbers in the apparel trades; English, Scotch, Polish, and

Germans and their descendants in the textile industries; Irish in building construction, transportation, and in municipal employment. The metal products industries draw from all nationality groups, although plants employing younger workers have predominantly American-born workers. Some highly skilled workers from Germany and the Scandinavian countries, however, are found in the metal-working industries. Though in earlier years many persons employed as domestic servants in Philadelphia came from Northern European countries, they have been increasingly replaced by Negroes in recent decades.

Two long-term trends have affected the age of the Philadelphia labor force. One is the decline in the proportion of workers under 21 years of age, and the other, a gradual aging of the population. Workers under 21 years of age were 18 per cent of all workers 10 years of age and over in 1910, but by 1950, when only persons 14 years of age and over were counted in the labor force, they had declined to 7.5 per cent of the city's labor force. A parallel decline occurred in the national labor force, although the proportion of children 10 to 13 years of age to the total was substantially higher in the nation than in Philadelphia in earlier decades.[5]

As a result of the postponement of entrance to the labor market on the part of young persons and a rise in the levels of education, the average years of schooling of the population have increased. A rough measure of the increase between 1910 and 1950 is found in a comparison of the schooling of persons who were 25 to 34 and 65 to 74 years of age in 1950. In Philadelphia, the average (median) years of schooling for the younger group was 11.4 school grades and for the older group, 8.1 grades or an increase of 3.3 grades. In the country as a whole, an increase of 3.8 school grades is found.[6]

Between 1910 and 1950, the median age of the city's population and labor force increased by five or more years. Men in the labor force in 1910 were, on the average (median), 35.3 years of age and, in 1950, 40.2 years. Women workers were 29.9 years old, on the

---

5 Between 1890 and 1940, the proportion of boys and girls from 14 to 19 years of age in the nation's labor force declined by a fourth and the average age of entrants to the labor market increased by about three years.—Durand, *op. cit.*, pp. 28-31.

6 Computed from *1950 Census of Population,* Vol. II, part 1, p. 236, and part 38, p. 284.

average, in 1910, and 36.6 in 1950. (Appendix Table 11) This aging of the labor force occurred during a period when, for reasons that will be discussed in a subsequent chapter, the hiring policy of employers and modifications of labor requirements as a result of technological changes favored the employment of younger workers.

In addition to the aging of the population and labor force during this period there was an increase in the potential length of retirement. It is estimated that during the first half of this century, the average amount of time spent by men in retirement has doubled. Despite longer periods of retirement and later entry into the labor force, the average length of working life for men has also increased, because of increasing longevity of the population.[7] These demographic changes occurred during a period in which there were substantial changes in the demand for goods and services in the economy that had far-reaching effects on the distribution of employment by industry and by occupation, both in the nation and in Philadelphia.

Changes in the Skills of the Experienced Labor Force

Partly as a result of the industrial shifts in employment noted in the preceding chapter and partly as a result of altered requirements within industries, the skills of the Philadelphia labor force changed considerably over the decades from 1910 to 1950. Appendix Table 12 presents data for experienced workers in the city's labor force for these decades on a basis comparable with the definitions of major occupational groups used in the 1950 Census of Population. During these four decades, there were several major groups that increased at a much more rapid rate than the total labor force, namely, professional and sales workers of both sexes, male operatives and service workers, and female clerical workers. Skilled craftsmen and foremen showed only a slight increase and managerial workers were more or less stationary, while the number of male laborers declined drastically. Most of the trends noted had started prior to 1930 but were more marked by 1950.

Practically stationary levels for the group of proprietors, managers, and officials, especially proprietors, were associated with a general decline in various types of self-employment and small business

[7] Seymour L. Wolfbein, "The Changing Length of Working Life," paper presented at annual meeting of Industrial Relations Research Association, December 29, 1954.

enterprise, particularly in trade and manufacturing. The decline in laborers was associated with changing skill requirements in manufacturing, construction, and transportation as well as with declining levels of employment in some segments of these industries. The numbers employed as craftsmen declined both absolutely and relatively after World War I as a result of changes in labor requirements and declines in total employment in the industries that usually engage a substantial number of skilled workers. Clerical, sales, and professional workers were attached to industries in which employment was increasing and to occupations that were in greater demand by reason of increased "paper work" in the conduct of all types of business, and a higher degree of specialization in particular activities.

Proportionate gains between 1910 and 1950 were greater for women than for men in the case of professional, clerical, and sales workers. Among service workers and operatives, on the other hand, net increases were relatively higher for men than for women. A decline in domestic service occupations was associated with increasing commercialization of activities that had formerly been performed in homes, the introduction of labor-saving devices of all sorts in housework, and new patterns of family living. In addition, a decline in the supply of foreign-born domestic servants in all probability also affected this trend.

Remnants of the handicrafts were more heavily represented in the 1910 than in the 1950 labor force. Dressmakers and tailors gave way to factory operatives. Substantial numbers of coachmen, teamsters, harness makers, livery stable workers, and carriage and wagon builders in 1910 had been replaced by chauffeurs, truck and taxi drivers, gas station attendants, garage mechanics, and employees in automobile factories. In both the city and the nation, the general nature of occupational changes took the form of reducing the demand for heavy manual work in homes, factories, and other business activities and of increasing the specialization of labor.

The ranking of individual occupational groups in the labor force was also altered between 1910 and 1950, both locally and nationally. (Appendix Table 13) Operatives continued to remain the largest single group in both the city and the nation. Craftsmen dropped from second to third place in the city, but remained in second place in the nation. Perhaps the most significant changes in the structure of employment are reflected in the shift of laborers from second to eighth rank in the nation and of clerical workers from fifth to second rank in the city. The proportion of all white-collar workers to the total rose by about ten percentage points in both the city and the nation.

Local changes in the proportion of women to the total employed in each occupational group tended to correspond with national changes. The proportion of women to the total increased substantially in clerical and sales occupations, both locally and nationally. By 1950, women constituted nearly two-thirds of all workers in clerical occupations.

In other types of occupations in which substantial numbers of women have been employed, such as service workers and operatives, relatively fewer women were employed in 1950 than in 1910. Nevertheless, in 1950, women constituted over a half of all service workers in both the city and the nation and 36 and 28 per cent, respectively, of all operatives. Women as a proportion of all professional and related workers gained slightly in Philadelphia but lost in the nation between 1910 and 1950.

The significance of occupational trends between 1910 and 1950 is clarified if employment changes are viewed in the light of the size of the populations concerned. (Chart 4, Appendix Table 14) It will be recalled that there were ten per cent fewer persons at work in Philadelphia in 1950 than in 1910, relative to its population at both dates, while employment in nonfarm occupations compared to nonfarm population in the nation had declined by five per cent. Except for operatives and kindred workers, the direction of local employment trends for both sexes paralleled those of the nation. White-collar workers increased except for managers, proprietors, and officials, while manual groups, except operatives (in the United States), declined. The greatest decline occurred among laborers. In the nation, the increase in nonfarm employment was highest in clerical work while in Philadelphia it was highest in professional and related occupations. Local employment of craftsmen declined more drastically and that of sales workers increased more rapidly than in the nation.

For each 10,000 persons in the populations compared, gross changes in employment resulted in a net loss in the city of 722 jobs in some occupational groups and a gain of 302 jobs in others, compared with

CHART 4—Percentage Change in Employment Relative to Population by Major Occupation Groups, Philadelphia and the United States, 1910-1950

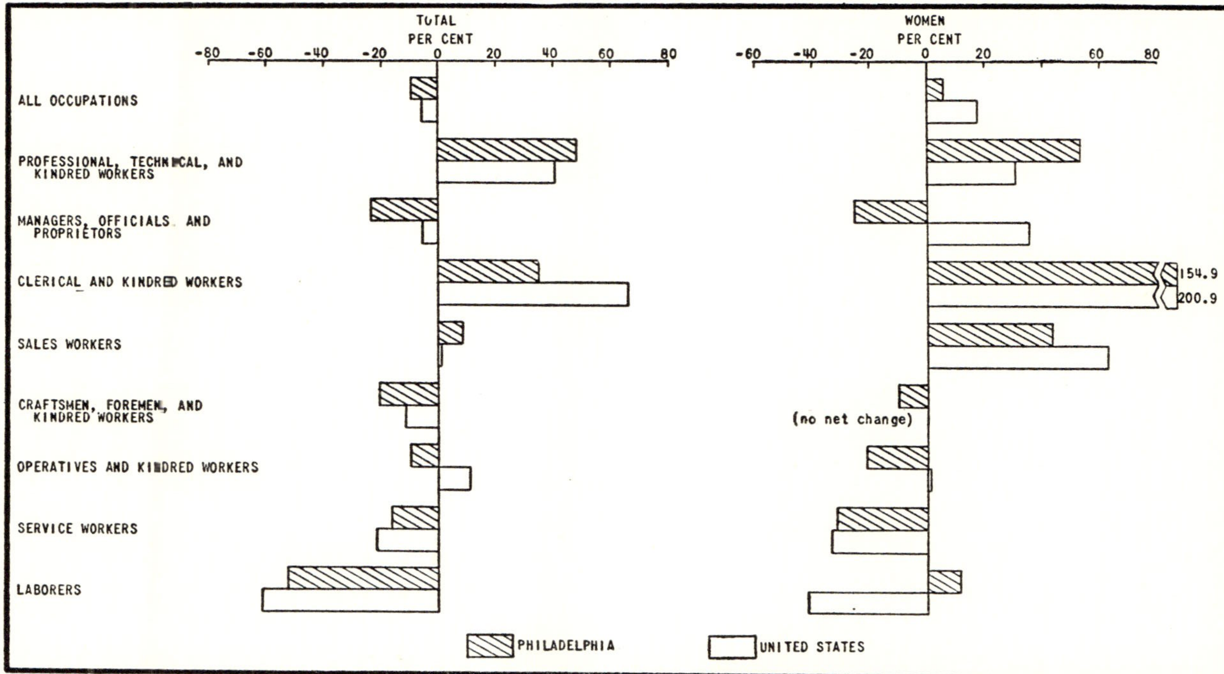

SOURCE: Appendix table 14

a net loss of 644 jobs and a gain of 426 jobs in the nation.[8] The vast majority of the declines occurred in manual occupations. If one can assume that changes in skill requirements within industries tend to affect all areas alike, then differences in employment trends between the nation and Philadelphia, as in operatives, reflect changes in the demand for the labor of the city's residents and hence modifications in the economic base.

In the context of changes in employment that take account of the size of the populations concerned, the employment of women gained less rapidly in the city than in the nation between 1910 and 1950. If one excludes from consideration the small numbers of women employed as craftsmen and laborers, the direction of local occupational trends parallel those in nonfarm occupations for the nation as a whole, except in the case of managerial workers and operatives. Gains in women's employment were greater in local than in national professional occupations, but other gains were smaller. The shift from manual to nonmanual types of work that characterized these decades was even more pronounced for women than for men.

Mobility of the Labor Force

Measures of net changes in levels of skill between 1910 and 1950 understate the amount of occupational shifting that took place during this period. There were additional types of changes within the broad occupational groups used here, as well as shifts from decade to decade and from year to year within a decade. Many occupational changes, such as those in the expanding clerical, sales, and professional occupations, were effectuated by the recruitment to new jobs of young workers who had received appropriate training. In some instances of declining opportunity, workers who retired were not replaced; in others, they transferred to other jobs. In addition, many experienced workers were laid off and forced to look elsewhere for jobs or make changes in their occupational or industrial attachments on their own initiative. Voluntary shifts were much more characteristic of the decades preceding the thirties and in the forties, while involuntary shifts and unemployment increased between 1930 and 1940.

---

8 Computed from Appendix Table 14.

No data are available to measure the degree and kinds of mobility of the city's labor force over the entire period under review. The geographic mobility of the population in the two decades after World War I has already been noted. Studies of the work histories of selected groups in the city's labor force and other data provide clues to the direction of job shifts and the characteristics of the persons who changed jobs. Little is known, however, about variations in the degree of labor mobility that accompany changes in the levels of business activity or in the structure of the economy. Labor turnover in the nation's manufacturing industries was higher in the twenties and the forties than in the thirties,[9] and it may be assumed that mobility in the sense of change of occupation, industry, or place of residence was higher in these periods in industrial centers like Philadelphia.

The impact of the changes in the structure of employment discussed in this and the preceding chapter emerged more clearly during the depression of the thirties. In 1936, sample surveys were made of workers in local industries in which employment had expanded prior to that date and in occupations of declining importance or in which major changes had occurred in labor requirements. These studies procured the previous work experience records from 1926 to 1936 and, in most cases, lifetime work histories.[10]

This evidence indicates that although some workers did transfer from declining to expanding industries, they were likely to be a selected group in terms of age and sex. In the hosiery industry, for example, which had expanded up to 1929, over half of the hosiery workers studied in 1936 had come from other industries.[11] This proportion was higher for knitters, who are men, than for women employed as toppers, seamers, and loopers. More women than men had come directly into the industry from school and over 40 per cent of all workers attached to the industry in 1936 had experience *only* in this industry. Although a wide range of other industries was repre-

9 W. S. Woytinsky, *Three Aspects of Labor Dynamics* (Washington: Social Science Research Council, 1942), chaps. III-V.

10 Summarized in E. Wight Bakke *et al.*, *Labor Mobility and Economic Opportunity* (New York: John Wiley and Sons and The Technology Press of Massachusetts Institute of Technology, 1954), chap. 3.

11 This statement is based on unpublished data from the Industrial Research Department unemployment sample of 1936 for full-fashioned hosiery workers for whom work histories were obtained.

sented in the previous experience of the workers who had transferred to the hosiery industry, manufacturing experience predominated. About 10 per cent of the total attached to this industry in 1936 were predominantly younger workers who came from other textile industries.

Parallel findings are indicated in the results of a sample survey of workers attached to the radio industry, an industry that expanded in the late twenties and early thirties.[12] It, too, recruited workers from other industries, particularly toolmakers, but they were younger than the average toolmaker in the city. The proportion of workers recruited directly to the radio industry without previous work experience was relatively high. In this industry also, men were comparatively more mobile than women, and over a fourth of the women and eight per cent of the men attached to the industry in 1936 were former textile workers.

Because the decline in textile employment was unusually severe during the period under review, the mobility of textile workers warrants special consideration. It is well known that they have a strong sense of attachment to the industry and that their skills are not readily transferable.[13] Over four-fifths of Philadelphia weavers studied in 1936 had entered the labor market prior to 1920, a majority having entered before 1910.[14] Men in this group had averaged 18 1/2 years of weaving experience and women, 15 years. Transfers to other occupations from this group were relatively few in number unless forced by a prolonged layoff. Even then, there was a tendency for weavers to consider themselves attached to the textile industry. One weaver expressed a common view in the course of an interview, when he said that although he considered that the textile industry was "shot in Philadelphia," and would not want his children to get into it, he himself would stay because "it's a trade that

---

12 Gladys L. Palmer and Ada M. Stoflet, *The Labor Force of the Philadelphia Radio Industry in 1936*, Report No. P-2 (Philadelphia: WPA National Research Project in cooperation with the Industrial Research Department, University of Pennsylvania, 1938).

13 Gladys L. Palmer, "Mobility of Weavers in Three Textile Centers," *Quarterly Journal of Economics*, May 1941, pp. 460-87.

14 Gladys L. Palmer, *Ten Years of Work Experience of Philadelphia Weavers and Loomfixers*, Report No. P-4 (Philadelphia: WPA National Research Project in cooperation with Industrial Research Department, University of Pennsylvania, 1938).

gets into you."[15] By 1936, of course, many former weavers had retired from the labor market or had already transferred to other industries, such as radio and hosiery manufacture. Nevertheless, the strong sense of attachment to the industry that characterized workers in this period had prevailed for a long time. The weavers studied in 1936 had shifted from product to product or from one employer to another, but had seldom changed their occupation except when moving to weaving from a less skilled operation. Among weavers, men had been more mobile than women and younger workers more mobile than older workers. For a variety of reasons, including their relatively high average age and a strong sense of attachment to the industry, weavers had stayed with their looms.

The history of the textile industry in the city had been such that as one branch of the industry declined, another expanded. When woolen and worsted production was expanding, weavers moved into this field from other textile branches. Similar transfers occurred when upholstery weaving expanded and woolen and worsted weaving declined. There was, therefore, a basis in previous experience for workers' believing that some branch of textiles would eventually pick up, even if the particular branch in which they were engaged was declining. The persistent downward swing of employment in all branches of the local woven goods industry for most of the years after 1929 was without parallel in their relatively long experience.

Structural changes in the local economy had also occurred in the metal-products industries, as noted previously. Specifically, these took the form of contracting employment opportunity after World War I in the plants with heavy processing operations, particularly in iron and steel mills and plants producing railroad and streetcar equipment. Employment in communications equipment and other segments of the lighter metal industries increased. The hiring specifications for machinists in the two types of metal-processing industries differed. There is evidence from the work records studied in 1936[16] that the workers recruited to the machinists' trade after World War I secured jobs primarily in the lighter metal industries.

---

15 *Ibid.*, p. 3.

16 Helen Herrmann, *Ten Years of Work Experience of Philadelphia Machinists,* Report No. P-5 (Philadelphia: WPA National Research Project in cooperation with Industrial Research Department, University of Pennsylvania, 1938), and unpublished tabulations.

Moreover, relatively few from the heavy industries shifted to lighter products and, as a group, they experienced more unemployment between 1926 and 1936 than maintenance machinists or than production machinists in the lighter metal industries. In general, the younger men were more mobile than older machinists.

All of these studies indicate that the Philadelphia labor force made adjustments to the structural changes that were occurring in the local economy. Significant proportions of workers were recruited to the expanding occupations and industries directly from school. In addition, younger workers with experience succeeded in shifting from declining to expanding segments of the economy. Older workers were less successful in making such transfers and their experience, particularly after 1930, reflected a downgrading of skill level on jobs, substantial periods of unemployment, or retirement from the labor market. However, age was not a handicap to those workers whose jobs were not involved in large-scale layoffs or complete shutdowns. The net effect of this pattern of shifts was that the average age of men and women in the expanding industries was considerably lower, and of workers in contracting industries considerably higher, than the average for men and women in the city's labor force as a whole. This growing differential in age resulted in an increasing rate of retirement in contracting industries and occupations.

A study of the Philadelphia labor force in 1951, covering a sample of work histories for the decade, 1940 to 1950, substantiated many of the findings of the earlier studies.[17] There were, for example, more voluntary shifts and more shifts that were advantageous to the individual in the periods when employment was relatively high. With the same exposure to the labor market, younger workers were found to be more mobile than older workers and men than women. Manual workers were more mobile than nonmanual. In general, the rate of accessions to contracting industries was low. Expanding industries and occupations gained as a result of shifts of experienced workers from other activities and the recruitment of inexperienced workers. The only exception occurred in the case of professional occupations in

[17] Unpublished data from the Survey of Patterns and Factors in Labor Mobility, 1940-1950, which was summarized in Gladys L. Palmer, *Labor Mobility in Six Cities* (New York: Social Science Research Council, 1954).

which expansion was primarily the result of training a new labor supply. Despite rapid increases in employment between 1940 and 1950 and the effect of wartime manpower controls that induced certain types of job shifts, a majority of Philadelphia workers were found to have had stable attachments to particular occupations or types of work over the decade. As in earlier decades, a relatively small proportion of workers was responsible for a disproportionate number of the job changes made between 1940 and 1950. Some of the data from this study will be discussed in greater detail subsequently, but it may be noted at this point that although a metropolitan labor force responds both to the opportunity to move and to circumstances that force a change, its response to the former is more rapid and usually more rewarding for the individuals concerned.

Implications of Labor-Force Changes

Trends in the size and composition of the Philadelphia labor force and its occupational distribution have been discussed in some detail in this chapter. The major developments may be summarized by contrasting the character of the labor force in 1910 and 1950. In the "horse and buggy" days of 1910, the city was a compact labor market and most workers were employed in the neighborhoods where they lived. By 1950, improved transportation facilities made it possible for workers to commute over greater distances and the dispersion of plant locations and movement of the population to surrounding suburbs widened the geographic area of the city's labor market to include neighboring communities.

The city's population in 1950 differed in several respects from that in 1910. Only 16 per cent of the population was 45 years of age or over in 1910, while in 1950, this proportion had risen to 31 per cent. One in every four persons was foreign-born in 1910, but this ratio had dropped to one in ten by 1950. In the meantime, the proportion of nonwhite (predominantly Negro) to the total population had risen from 6 to over 18 per cent.

Local production of goods and services in 1910 was dependent on a substantial amount of labor by children and young people. By 1950, however, compulsory education laws and the longer schooling that accompanied rising standards of living had led to a postponement of labor-force participation by young people and the virtual abolition of child labor. These developments, together with the aging of the city's population, added several years to the average age of men and women in the labor force over the four decades. Although the proportion of all women who were in the labor force was only slightly higher in 1950 than in 1910, women's employment was relatively more significant in the later period because of a decline in the proportion of the male population in the labor force.

The occupational distribution of Philadelphia's labor force in 1950 also differed from that in 1910. Professional, clerical, sales, and kindred workers were relatively more important in the city's labor force in the later than in the earlier period. These changes indirectly reflected increased employment opportunity for white-collar wage and salary workers and stationary or declining opportunity in the skilled crafts, unskilled labor, and in various types of self-employment or small business enterprise. Relative to national occupational patterns, Philadelphia was still a major center for the skilled crafts and for machine operators experienced on a variety of equipment, but this position was less marked in 1950 than it had been in 1910.

Between these two dates, large numbers of foreign immigrants and of Negroes from the southern states had entered the city's labor force at relatively low grades of skill. Nevertheless, the general socioeconomic status of the occupations of the total labor force was raised during the period. While this improvement in status was probably more effective for native-born white residents or the second generation of immigrants, it was a concomitant of a general rise in standards of living and of changes in knowledge and skill throughout the nation.

When one takes account of the increase in population over this period, local trends in the employment opportunity for manual workers did not differ substantially from national shifts in the nonagricultural segment of the economy, except in the case of operatives and kindred workers. The demand for professional and for sales workers increased at a more rapid rate locally than nationally, but that for clerical workers at a less rapid rate. The decline in managerial workers was greater in Philadelphia than in the nation. Since it may be assumed that local shifts in the skill requirements of industry followed national patterns, such differences as there were in local and national occupational trends were associated with variations in the rate of decline of manufacturing or the rate of growth in nonmanufacturing industries as between the city and the nation.

In the past, it has been assumed that most of the major shifts required of a labor force in adapting to broad structural changes in the economy over several decades can be accomplished by the recruitment of young workers to new or expanding fields of employment and the gradual retirement of workers in declining industries. The rapidity and extent of the structural changes that occurred in Philadelphia between 1910 and 1950, however, required more than the redirection of the employment of young workers. Substantial numbers of experienced workers also made occupational and industrial changes, left the area for jobs in other communities, or retired from the labor market. In general, younger workers were more successful in making the necessary occupational and industrial shifts than older workers and those with readily transferable skills, such as machinists and toolmakers, than workers in such occupations as weaving and loomfixing. The adaptability or mobility of the community's labor force thus became an important factor during this period of substantial changes in the structure of employment.

The raising of the age of compulsory education during a period of rapid shifts in composition of the population created special problems for the public educational program. These problems were enhanced by a concomitant decline in relative opportunities for employment in the skilled crafts after World War I and by relatively low rates of increase in semiskilled occupations. Full advantage was taken of increasing opportunities for clerical and sales workers in the city's educational program, but this did not necessarily solve vocational training problems for Negroes and some nationality groups who were precluded from consideration for the majority of clerical and selling jobs by employer's hiring specifications. At the same time, there was a decline in the demand for unskilled labor and domestic servants, occupations that usually employ substantial numbers of Negroes, during a period when the proportion of Negroes in the population was rising.

A significant aging of the population occurred in a period when employers' hiring specifications favored younger workers. The consequences of this development will be discussed in greater detail in the following chapter, but attention may be drawn at this point to the contraction in employment opportunity for proprietors during these decades, because they are an occupational group that normally includes substantial numbers of older workers. The numbers of women in the labor force increased over two-fifths during these decades, and, relative to population changes, their employment increased in nonmanual but declined in manual occupations. This development was followed by changes in the city's vocational training programs for girls that shifted emphasis from the "trades" to white-collar occupations.

One of the outstanding developments of this span of four decades was a growing uncertainty about where a worker might expect to earn a livelihood over a lifetime. Up to 1920, manufacturing employment had consistently expanded in the Philadelphia area, and although there were occasional periods of over-all decline during a depression, an experienced worker could find another job relatively easily, if the plant in which he had been employed closed or employment in his particular branch of an industry declined. Between 1920 and 1930, however, total employment in manufacturing dropped below the levels of 1910. Employment in the service industries increased, but this expansion occurred largely in professional, semiprofessional, and clerical occupations, the educational requirements for which differed from those in the mechanical pursuits. Then came a prolonged depression that reduced levels of employment in all industries. Meanwhile, technological changes modified the labor requirements of some industries and many plants began training young workers on the job rather than recruiting experienced ones from other industries. All of these developments led to job insecurity and to an undermining of the prestige-value of apprenticeship training and craftsmanship in the community. A growing sense of insecurity among workers with respect to the channels of lifetime employment was accompanied by an actual increase in the length of the lifespan and of potential retirement or old-age dependency.

The changes in the population and the demand for labor that characterized the period between World Wars I and II might have created no special problems if the local economy had been operating at high levels of employment throughout the interim. But long-term declines in some industries and occupations started in the twenties, and the decade from 1930 to 1940 was one of persistent depression interrupted by only short periods of recovery. Under the unremitting economic strains that affected all groups in the community, these longer-term trends took on greater significance. The effects on labor-market operations of a decade of unemployment are discussed in greater detail in the next chapter.

Chapter V

The Effects of a Severe and Prolonged Depression on the Labor Market

THE HISTORY of unemployment in a community is the story of the effects of periodic malfunctioning of the economy in terms of substantial amounts of unrealized production, unused labor, and reduced income. The increasing severity of various depressions during the years from 1910 to 1940 was reflected not only in the numbers of job-seekers in the city of Philadelphia (and the nation) but also in the character of public discussion about the unemployment problem. The depression of 1907, for example, did not appear to have serious effects in the city, but that of 1913 to 1915 resulted in substantial unemployment and the beginnings of wide public interest in the problem. It was at this time that discussion focused on reducing frictions in the labor market, that is to say, on methods of stabilizing and regularizing employment, particularly the role that might be played by employers in this respect; on the values of a public employment service for facilitating the marketing process; and on the need for record-keeping by employers and the community with regard to employment and unemployment. The latter half of the decade from 1910 to 1920 was marked by the first appearance of local public employment exchanges, and labor-market experience during World War I led to increased attention on the part of employers to the "costs" of high labor turnover and the advantages of centralized personnel practices and employment record-keeping.

There was a short but severe depression in 1921-1922 that had been preceded by substantial declines in employment in local shipbuilding and munitions industries at the close of World War I. The decade from 1920 to 1930 as a whole, however, was relatively prosperous.

Many technological improvements with resulting changes in labor requirements were introduced and there were shifts in the demand for labor in specific industries and for manual relative to white-collar workers. Some workers found it difficult to make the necessary adaptations and toward the end of the period, public interest was aroused by the concurrence of relatively high levels of employment and an increasing volume of unemployment. Simultaneously, interest developed in vocational guidance and training programs as a means of assisting young people in making adjustments in the labor market and in unemployment insurance as an offset to loss of income after layoffs. The personnel policies of employers became increasingly important as an institutional force in the labor market during this period.

The decade from 1930 to 1940 was marked by severe and prolonged depression throughout the country and Philadelphia was no exception. The longer-term declines in certain segments of the local economy that had started before and after World War I were accentuated. Levels of local factory employment, even in the relatively prosperous years of the period, did not reach the levels of 1929, let alone those of 1919 or 1909. The volume of part-time employment and unemployment increased after 1929 until, in the spring of 1933, only a little over a third of the city's labor force was employed full-time. Declining wage rates and part-time employment resulted in substantial losses of earning power to the workers who had jobs. Sheriff's sale signs on workers' homes and closed stores, banks, stock brokers' offices, and factories testified to the economic losses of all groups in the community.

The development of Federal relief programs and public works, the National Recovery Administration, and the Social Security program provided some offsets to the losses that workers and the community would otherwise have sustained during this decade. Nevertheless, many skilled workers with years of experience were forced to take any jobs they could get and other workers suffered the demoralizing effects of months and years of unemployment. Hiring specifications of employers became highly selective with regard to education, experience, race, age, sex, and other qualifications. One of the major misfortunes of the period was a high rate of unemployment among young persons entering the labor market. Although unemployment in the latter half of the decade was less severe than in the first half, it was of signally long duration, and was measured in months and years, rather than in weeks, as in 1930, or in days, as in 1910. The decade was characterized by a substantial out-migration from Philadelphia to other areas, but even so, as the depression continued, there developed a "hard core" of long-term unemployed, who were not absorbed into employment until there were marked increases in the demand for labor as a result of the production requirements of World War II.

Discussion of unemployment problems focused first on whether there was a problem and its magnitude and then on need for public aid. It took several years of severe depression to modify the community attitudes that underlie the phrases, "some folks won't work" and "anyone who really wants to work can find a job." Eventually, however, the quest for security against unemployment characterized almost all groups in the population and public attitudes changed with regard to the need for an unemployment insurance program. Concomitant with this development was the general acceptance of two ideas: (1) mass unemployment was a social misfortune and not a personal disgrace for the individuals affected; and (2) programs developed by individual employers to stabilize or regularize employment had distinct limitations when the total demand for labor was not sufficient to employ the labor force. In other words, it was recognized that mass unemployment was essentially a social problem that had to be alleviated by broad public policies. Its magnitude and duration were affected primarily by the strengths and weaknesses of the entire economy rather than by the production policies of individual employers or the specific qualifications of individual job-seekers.

In outlining what was learned about severe and prolonged unemployment during the depression of the thirties in Philadelphia, several considerations require emphasis. One is the effect of such a depression on the nature of labor-market transactions. Another is the effect on labor-force participation, that is to say, the general question of whether during a depression the net size of the labor force and hence, the numbers of unemployed, is swelled by job-seekers who are not normally in the labor market but whose entrance is occasioned by the loss of jobs by other family members. An additional consideration is the effect of persistent depression on the characteristics of the job-seekers, since there is a tendency toward a "crystallization" of the unemployment problem in a prolonged depression. Here, "crystallization" is used to describe the process by which a group of unemployed persons is divided into those who are reabsorbed into jobs relatively quickly and those who come in time to constitute a "hard core" of long-time unemployed. Finally, the incidence of unemployment in families, as distinct from its incidence among individuals, is important in a consideration of its social impact and costs. The following pages summarize this experience for Philadelphia, with some comparative data for the nation.

PHILADELPHIA'S RATES OF UNEMPLOYMENT

In earlier days, unemployment was often likened to the Irishman's leaking roof about which nothing needed to be done when the sun was shining, and about which nothing could be done once the rain had started. This was essentially the case even with respect to information about the numbers out of work. It was the experience of the winters of 1914-15 and of 1921-22 that first stimulated the interest of cities in data about local unemployment. Although the Censuses of Population of 1880, 1890, 1900, and 1910 had secured some information on job-seekers, more specific and useful questions were asked in the census of 1930 and in special censuses in 1931 and 1937. Several cities, notably Buffalo, Cincinnati, and Philadelphia had experimented with annual sample surveys taken in conjunction with school censuses. It was not until the end of the depression, however, that a series of monthly reports on the work status of a sample of the national population became available. Although many of these experiments in direct measurement of the work status of the population started as surveys of unemployment, their eventual uses were found to cover all aspects of changing labor-force composition and work status.

The rates of unemployment for Philadelphia (Chart 5, Appendix Table 15) were obtained by direct measurement of the work status of the population in sample surveys[1] and in Censuses of Population in

1 The Industrial Research Department sample that was used from 1929 to 1938 was a selection of School Blocks from the School Census Districts. The Blocks

CHART 5—Employment Status of Philadelphia Workers at Selected Dates, 1929-1950

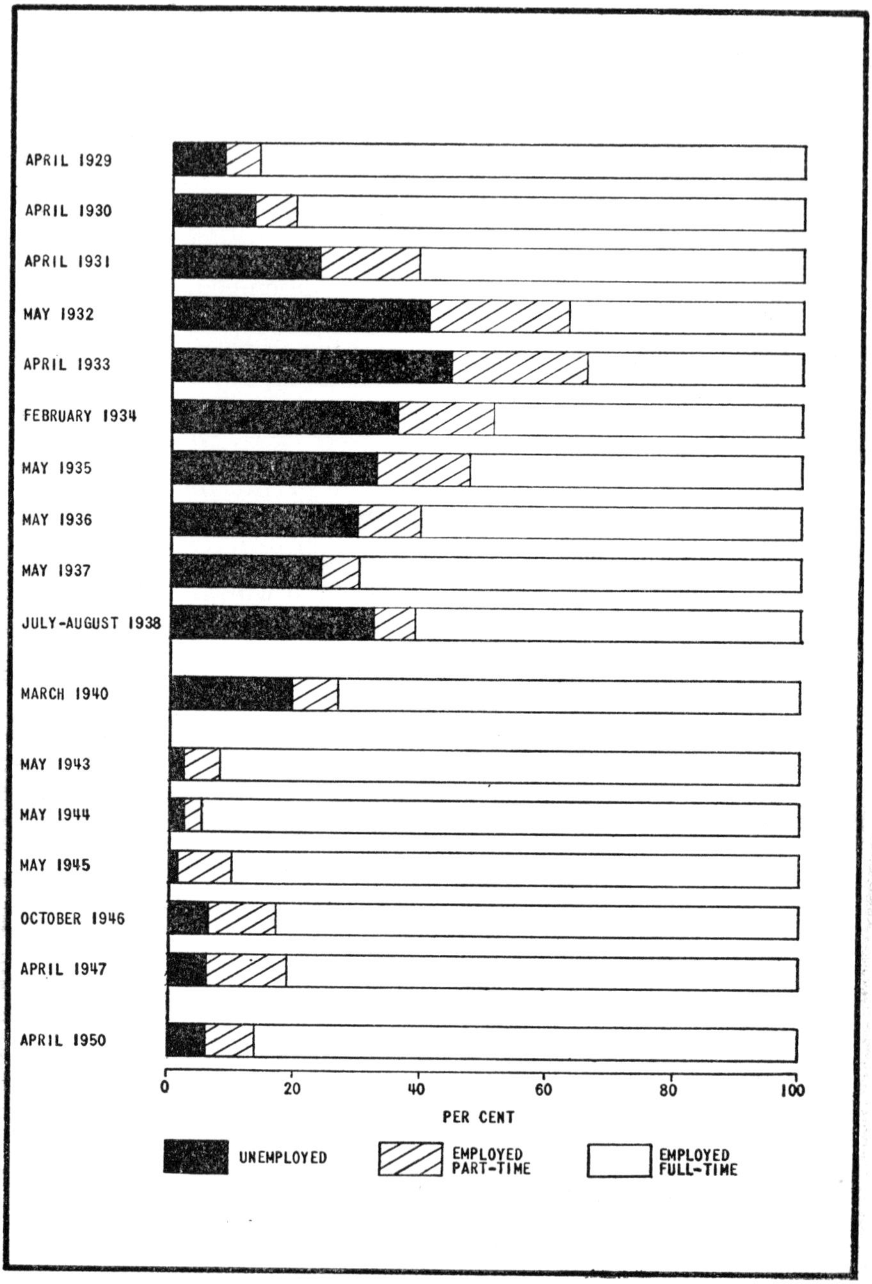

SOURCE: Appendix table 15

a given month for 17 out of 21 years from 1929 to 1950. During this period, the rate of unemployment in Philadelphia was higher than for nonfarm workers in the country as a whole, and in the worst years it was substantially higher than the national rate. (Appendix Table 16) There is reason to believe that unemployment rates in Philadelphia from 1929 to 1938 are overstated in relation to those of later years, largely because of a difference in concepts used. In the earlier period, the interviewer classified persons as unemployed who were not at work on the *day* of enumeration but were "able and willing to work," whereas in the later years, work status was measured for a given *week* and looking for work became the major criterion of classification in doubtful cases.[2]

---

were chosen to yield representative income levels and race and nationality coverage of the population, as well as geographic distribution. (For further details on original sampling design, see J. F. Dewhurst and E. A. Tupper, *Social and Economic Characteristics of Unemployment in Philadelphia, April 1929*, U. S. Bureau of Labor Statistics, Bulletin No. 520, June 1930.) The original sampling design was modified in 1930, and from 1931 to 1938 identical blocks were enumerated each year, except for three substitutions. The enumerating facilities varied from year to year and the number of schedules therefore varied. The use of a fixed sample of approximately 45,000 households for the period covered had certain analytical advantages, but may have led to the introduction of some biases. Although the size of the city's population was practically the same in 1940 as in 1930, its composition had changed and its size had fluctuated during the decade. Shifts of residence within the city led to a slight overweighting for Negro population in the sample blocks by 1938. This sample design was less efficient and subject to greater bias than the sampling designs developed in 1939 and 1940. After the 1940 Census of Population, the Industrial Research Department cooperated with the Bureau of the Census in enlarging the Philadelphia segment of the national Current Population Survey sample to secure labor-force and related estimates for the city in 1943 and 1944. The same type of sample was used by the Bureau of the Census in special surveys in 1945, 1946, and 1947.

2 The original work-status data secured in the Industrial Research Department sample surveys from 1929 to 1938 have been adjusted to obtain greater comparability with data for 1940 and later years and therefore differ slightly from previously published data. The adjustments were concentrated on the relatively small group reported as "temporarily not at work because of illness," based on data secured in each survey year. Despite this adjustment, the unemployment concept used from 1929 to 1938, "able and willing to work," might be expected to yield a larger affirmative response than the questions on "actively seeking work" or "looking for work" used in 1940 and subsequent years. A special check in an experimental sample on the results of adding a question on activity in seeking work (and reason for not seeking) following the question on ability and willingness to work showed that 4 per cent of those who were able and willing to work were inactive job-seekers in 1939. The size of the group of inactive unemployed might be expected to vary with the volume of unemployment, and no adjustment has been attempted for this overstatement. In addition, the work-status information secured from 1929 to 1938

In addition to persons who were without jobs, a fifth of the Philadelphia labor force was working part time in 1932 and 1933 and most of these workers can be assumed to have been available for full time work. As the demand for labor increased, its first impact was to reduce the number of persons on part time and to increase the amount of full-time work. In 1937 and 1938, for example, the rate of part-time work in the labor force was at levels comparable with those of more prosperous years. Part-time work is a method of work-sharing during a depression, and to the extent that it is above the levels in prosperous years it includes involuntary elements. On the basis of this record for Philadelphia, one can assume that any part-time work above a level of roughly 6 per cent of the labor force reflects partial unemployment, so that the figures for persons without jobs understate the amount of work lost by a labor force in a depression.

Character of Labor-Market Transactions

Labor-market transactions take place on a job-by-job basis. The demand for labor is in terms of specific job categories while the labor supply is composed of persons with specific kinds of skill and experience and differing personal attributes. Even with a large surplus of labor in a city, the specifications for a particular job opening and the qualifications of individual job-seekers will not always match. There were alleged "shortages"of labor in Philadelphia even during the depression. Certain types of coppersmith work, for example, for which there had been no demand in the area since the close of World War I, were in demand during one spurt of naval construction activity. It happened that all of the applicants with the required experience were over 60 years of age, but they were finally accepted, since no younger men were trained for the work. At the peak of the busy season in a few industries sporadic shortages were also reported. These "shortages" however, were temporary and did not, in any

referred to status on the *day* of enumeration and would presumably yield a different count of unemployed than status as of the *week* of enumeration (1940-1950). It is probable, therefore, that the data presented overstate unemployment in Philadelphia between 1929 and 1938 in relation to the data for subsequent years. Whatever the "true" unemployment rates may have been in these years, the trends within this period and the relationship discussed in the text are not affected.

event, affect enough persons to make a dent in the volume of unemployment.

The rigidity of hiring specifications fluctuates inversely with the looseness of the labor market. In periods of expanding demand for labor or of labor shortages, hiring specifications are relaxed, but in times of labor surplus they are more stringent and frequently become artificial. There was not only a dearth of job openings in Philadelphia during the depression years but the jobs available offered relatively low wages and the hiring specifications were frequently highly restrictive.

Some examples of hiring practices during this period will suffice to illustrate the character of the job market at this time. A large furrier in the city listed a job opening with the public employment office for an experienced girl to act as a double-entry bookkeeper and take entire charge of the office. One of the major requirements for the job, however, was that the girl be a blonde and be able to model size 16 garments. Machinists were in demand in the city during the depression, but they had to be experienced on particular kinds of equipment. The help-wanted advertisements read: "must be experienced on 8-foot vertical boring mill, able to read blueprints and do precision tool work." In office, selling, and service jobs, personality and appearance requirements became stringent. One restaurant, newly established in the city during the depression, was staffed entirely by tall, willowy blondes without experience, while experienced waiters and waitresses walked the streets looking for jobs. Moreover, for many jobs educational specifications were raised and high school and college graduates were preferred to those without such education.[3]

One effect of hiring practices that aroused public attention was the disadvantageous position of the older worker. Discrimination against the older worker started in the twenties, probably as an indirect result of the introduction of insurance and pension plans in numerous business establishments and as a direct result of other developments. Technological changes occurring in the two decades

---

3 Examples cited in Gladys L. Palmer, *The Search for Work in Philadelphia, 1932-1936*, Report No. P-7 (Philadelphia: WPA National Research Project in cooperation with Industrial Research Department, University of Pennsylvania, 1939), p. 34.

modified the experience requirements for some jobs—many plants preferred to take young persons for training on the job rather than retrain older persons with more experience. The net effect of these developments was that expanding, mass production industries were increasingly staffed by young people, and, during the depression, experience and, more particularly, the age that goes with experience, were sometimes a disadvantage. In the words of a skilled weaver in Philadelphia who had been born in Lyons, France, "a man's years were respected in Europe because his training and experience were considered valuable" but in this country a man was "through" at 40 or 45 years of age.[4] Certain qualifications to these statements should be added. Age was not necessarily a handicap to a worker in the skilled crafts or in the professions, as it was in securing other types of work. Moreover, although many plants trained young persons for jobs in the early years of the depression, there came a time when experienced employees could be obtained at the same rates of pay as inexperienced and, then, young people without any job experience were also at a disadvantage. As the depression continued, therefore, unemployment rates rose for the youngest and oldest workers but were lower for workers in the intermediate age groups.

The preference for personal qualifications over experience in many types of jobs and discrimination against older workers had additional effects. Community attitudes to training and experience were changed by this development and young people began to question the desirability of learning a "trade" or of making sacrifices to gain experience when so many skilled workers were out of jobs. Business personnel policy, in effect, therefore aggravated a situation in which long-term trends were already at work to the disadvantage of certain groups in the labor force. The population and labor force had aged during this and the preceding decades and technological and other economic changes had already narrowed the employment opportunity for workers with a "trade."

For many years, both employers and workers in Philadelphia had accepted the idea that stability of work experience was desirable. It

---

[4] Cited in Gladys L. Palmer, *Recent Trends in Employment and Unemployment in Philadelphia*, Report No. P-1 (Philadelphia: WPA National Research Project in cooperation with Industrial Research Department, University of Pennsylvania, 1937), p. 24.

was not uncommon for a worker to spend all of his working life in the employ of one company, and relatively long terms of service characterized the experience of many workers.[5] The depression may have undermined this attitude. Long service with one employer was not a handicap if that employer stayed in business, but if he went out of business, his long-service workers found it difficult to secure other jobs. In general, workers with highly specialized experience were less readily re-employed than those with varied experience or alternate skills.[6]

Work Records of the Employed

Even with mass unemployment in a city, some workers have steady employment. In general, they are engaged in activities that are not sensitive to cyclical change or they have skills and experience that are peculiarly valuable to an employer and are protected by seniority rules. In sample studies of the work experience of machinists and toolmakers and of weavers and loomfixers in Philadelphia in 1936, for example, it was found that one-half of the machinists, toolmakers, and loomfixers did not report any continuous periods of unemployment lasting a month or more in the ten years from 1926 to 1935.[7] Many of those workers, however, were engaged on maintenance rather than production work. Other findings from these studies have been cited earlier, but the work records of machinists and toolmakers in the period from 1926 through 1935 indicate that the largest number of man-months of unemployment for the decade was reported by those who were usually engaged in the transportation equipment industry.[8] The decline of employment in this industry had

5 In 1937, for example, data on length of service on current jobs were obtained for some 60,000 persons in the Philadelphia sample, who were employed in May 1937. Despite a substantial group of short-service workers who had secured jobs within the year as employment opportunities increased in 1936 and 1937, over a third (34.5 per cent) had worked on current jobs for ten years or over, and 12.4 per cent of all employed persons had worked on their jobs for twenty years or more.—Unpublished data from 1937 sample survey.

6 Palmer, *Recent Trends*, p. 33.

7 *Ibid.*, pp. 28-30.

8 Helen Herrmann, *Ten Years of Work Experience of Philadelphia Machinists*, Report No. P-5 (Philadelphia: WPA National Research Project in cooperation with Industrial Research Department, University of Pennsylvania, 1938) p. 32. See also E. Wight Bakke, *et al.*, *Labor Mobility and Economic Opportunity* (New York: John Wiley and Sons and the Technology Press of Massachusetts Institute of Technology, 1954), chap. 3.

had significant results, for its labor requirements differed from those of other metal products industries in the city, and machinists (and other workers) experienced on the heavy products characteristic of the local industry were not always successful in shifting to lighter precision work. The local shift from heavy to light work in production therefore created special adjustment problems for a substantial group of workers whose major experience had been on railroad and other heavy transportation equipment. Similarly, textile workers found that their skills were not readily transferable and experienced prolonged unemployment or had to take other types of jobs, when textile employment declined.

Upon loss of their usual jobs, many workers secured other employment, but frequently at lower grades of skill. In addition to the work-history studies cited, there is indirect evidence to this effect from a comparison of the usual and current occupations of the labor force reported in a study made in 1934. The direction of such shifts in both Pennsylvania and Philadelphia took the form of net increases in operatives, service workers, and laborers, and net declines in professional, clerical, and skilled workers.[9] For the country as a whole, an analysis of the sample statistics obtained at the time of the 1940 Census of Population indicates that the net changes in major occupational groups from usual to current occupation for employed workers took the form of declines in professional workers, farmers and farm laborers, clerical workers, and craftsmen, and increases in service workers, proprietors, operatives, and nonfarm laborers.[10] Obviously, some unemployed workers in the nation used their savings to engage in small business enterprises during the depression, but many of those who secured wage jobs were employed at lower grades of skill than that in their usual employment. One might summarize both local and national developments in this regard by saying that the effect of the depression on the work experience of some persons was a downgrading of skill-class, because occupational and industrial shifts were forced upon them. In addition, other employed persons were deprived of opportunities for promotion

---

9 Pennsylvania State Emergency Relief Administration, *Census of Employables in Urban and Rural Nonfarm Areas in Pennsylvania, 1934* (Harrisburg, 1936), p. 29; and unpublished data in 1936 sample survey for Philadelphia.

10 Computed from *1940 Census of Population, The Labor Force (Sample Statistics), Usual Occupation*, pp. 39-41.

that would have been available under more prosperous conditions.

Labor-Force Participation

In a depressed period some workers who are laid off may retire from the labor market; and nonworkers who had planned to enter the labor market may continue in school and postpone job-seeking until more jobs are available. Both of these developments tend to reduce the number of job-seekers. On the other hand, the total number of job-seekers may be increased by the entrance to the labor market of persons who are not normally wage earners but who are forced to seek jobs because of the unemployment of another member of the family.

Few data are available to measure the net effect of all of the changes in labor-force participation that occur during a depression. The data for Philadelphia indicate two types of developments that appeared to offset each other during the thirties. One was a slow but substantial increase from year to year in the number and proportion of households in the sample reporting no member in the labor force and a decline in the proportion of households having more than one worker. The other was a persistent increase in the number of inexperienced workers, who constituted 2 per cent of the labor force and 5 per cent of the unemployed in 1932, and were 7 per cent of the labor force and 22 per cent of the unemployed by 1938. The numbers of inexperienced workers were affected by high rates of unemployment for young persons, as well as by the entrance into the labor market of older but inexperienced persons who may have been seeking jobs because of the unemployment of other family members. The range in the proportion of inexperienced workers to the total, however, was substantially higher in the latter part of the decade. There were also more women in the labor force in later than in earlier depression years.

According to the Censuses of Population, the proportion of the total population in the city's labor force was 46 per cent in both 1930 and 1940.[11] Between 1930 and 1933, the proportion of the Philadelphia sample population in the labor force ranged from 42 to 43 per cent and rose to 45 and 46 per cent from 1934 to 1938. The dif-

11 These percentages were derived after the data were adjusted for comparability of labor-force concepts and age coverage.

ferences between the sample and complete census counts would indicate that the sample survey understated labor-force participation in the earlier years of the depression.

In the absence of age information for nonworkers in the Industrial Research Department sample surveys for earlier years and of population estimates by age for Philadelphia in each year of the decade from 1930 to 1940, more refined measures of labor-force participation during the depression years are not available. Philadelphia's population suffered a net loss of approximately 80,000 persons by out-migration,[12] the greater part of which apparently occurred between 1935 and 1940.[13] The sex ratio and the age structure of the adult population during the depression were therefore affected by this out-migration. The evidence of slightly higher labor-force participation in the sample population in the later than in the earlier years of the depression is not conclusive. It suggests, however, that if there is any substantial derivative unemployment in a long depression there is a time-lag in its appearance. If a time-lag is characteristic, the question may be raised as to whether this phenomenon is associated primarily with extended duration of unemployment on the part of the chief breadwinners in families rather than with a large volume of layoffs. Analysis of the number of workers per family in relation to the duration of unemployment of the chief wage earner, however, gives no support to the significance of this relationship.[14] It is more likely that in a prolonged depression the forces that tend to increase the number of persons seeking work for the first time are offset, or more than offset, by those that tend to encourage retirement or discourage entrance to the labor market and that, on balance, there is no significant increase in labor-force participation over time.[15] This is not to deny that, at any given time, there may be job-seekers whose entrance or re-entrance to the labor market is caused by the

12 Simon S. Kuznets, *The Population of Philadelphia and Environs*, Part I of a report to the City Planning Commission (Philadelphia: Institute of Local and State Government, University of Pennsylvania, 1946).

13 *1940 Census of Population, Internal Migration, 1935-1940, Social Characteristics of Migrant*, p. 220.

14 Unpublished data, 1936 and 1937 Philadelphia sample surveys.

15 For a contrary view, see W. S. Woytinsky, *Three Aspects of Labor Dynamics* (Washington: Social Science Research Council, 1942), chap. XV. The Philadelphia evidence on family employment patterns, used in Woytinsky's analysis, is open to another interpretation. See footnote 22 below. See also John D. Durand, *The Labor Force in the United States, 1890-1960* (New York: Social

unemployment of the usual breadwinner, but to indicate that their job-seeking may not be permanent or may be offset by withdrawals of regular wage earners from the labor market.

Characteristics of the Unemployed

There is some evidence in the Philadelphia surveys that at the beginning of a major depression, the characteristics of the unemployed do not differ markedly from those of the employed since large-scale layoffs are likely to occur by departments or plants. As a depression continues, however, selective hiring practices draw off certain groups from among the unemployed and the general characteristics of those not reabsorbed begin to differ substantially from those of the employed. Age, for example, did not appear to be a factor in the layoffs that took place early in the depression and, to the extent that seniority rules were a protection, older workers were less likely to be laid off. Nevertheless, once an older worker *was* laid off, his chances of re-employment diminished rapidly as the depression continued, because employers preferred to hire younger workers and could secure them readily.[16] Similarly, Negroes may not have been discriminated against in the original layoffs, but once unemployed, they were low on the preference lists for hirings. In the course of the depression, employers could secure experienced workers readily, and hence, the number and proportion of inexperienced job-seekers increased among the unemployed. As the depression continued, employers could choose workers from an unemployed pool that was being continuously augmented by some job turnover, by additional layoffs, and by the entrance into the labor market of young persons graduating from school and of other persons who began to look for work. Over the years, therefore, the characteristics of the unemployed came to differ from those of the employed, and the differences became particularly marked in the case of persons who had been unemployed for relatively long periods of time.

Science Research Council, 1948), pp. 100-2; Herbert G. Heneman, Jr., "Measurement of Secondary Unemployment: An Evaluation of Woytinsky's Methods," *Industrial and Labor Relations Review,* July 1950, pp. 567-74; and Clarence D. Long, "The Labor Force and Economic Change," chap. XIII in *Insights into Labor Issues* edited by Richard A. Lester and Joseph Shister (New York: The MacMillan Co., 1948) pp. 329-55.

An analysis of unemployment in Philadelphia in 1936 provides significant data with respect to the character of the unemployment problem about halfway through a decade of low employment levels. The demand for factory labor in Philadelphia was considerably higher in 1936 than at the low points in 1932 and 1933, but lower than the levels in 1937. Moreover, in 1936, average duration of unemployment had started to decline. Nevertheless, 30 per cent of the labor force was unemployed in May 1936 and the average experienced person looking for work had lost the last job at his usual occupation 28 months previously, and his last nonrelief job of one or more months' duration 21 months prior to the survey. A sixth of the total labor force had been looking for work for over a year. Among persons who had been unemployed for two or more years, the proportion of Negroes, of older workers, of workers in skilled and semi-skilled construction occupations, of laborers, and of men relative to women, was high.[17]

Some of these characteristics of the unemployed are related to longer-term changes in the population and labor force and in the demand for labor by occupation that were magnified by the effects of the depression. The aging of the population and labor force prior to 1936 made the risks of long-term unemployment greater for older workers who were laid off. A substantial decline in the demand for workers in the construction industry and for unskilled laborers generally accounted for a high incidence among workers usually engaged in these activities. Risks of long-term unemployment for Negroes were directly associated with a decline in the demand for unskilled labor and personal services, their predominant types of work, in relation to relatively rapid increases in their numbers in the Philadelphia population and labor force. It is also possible that an increase in the availability of whites for unskilled job openings and hiring

---

16 Sir William Beveridge, *Full Employment in a Free Society* (New York: W. W. Norton & Co., 1945), pp. 70-71, "The risk of losing one's job is much the same from 60 to 64 as it is from 35 to 44. . . . The risk of becoming chronically unemployed, that is to say of being out for more than a year, is two and a half times as great."

17 Gladys L. Palmer, *Employment and Unemployment in Philadelphia in 1936 and 1937*, Report No. P-3, Part I (Philadelphia: WPA National Research Project in cooperation with Industrial Research Department, University of Pennsylvania, 1938); and unpublished data from sample survey on which this study was based.

preferences for whites reduced the general rate of re-employment of Negroes.

Up to this point there has been no mention of the relation of industry trends in employment to the characteristics of the unemployed. It will be recalled that the layoffs from 1929 to 1933 and prior declines in local employment followed distinct industrial patterns, more workers being separated from some industries than from others. The resulting unemployment did not affect workers at random; on the contrary, it is reasonable to assume that most of the layoffs occurred by department or by occupation and that workers in the less specialized occupations were disemployed first. The gradual differentiation of the unemployed from the employed and of the long-term from the short-term unemployed that occurs during a prolonged depression appears to have followed occupational rather than industrial channels in Philadelphia. The only exception to this was in the construction industry. It is possible, but unlikely, that the wide diversification of manufacturing activities in Philadelphia obscured a more marked differentiation of the unemployed by industry.

Long-Term Unemployment

The year 1935 marked the highest level of long-term unemployment in Philadelphia, as measured from the date of loss of the last job at the usual occupation in the years from 1929 to 1934 and from loss of the last nonrelief job lasting a month or more, in the years from 1935 to 1939. Between 1929 and 1935 average duration of unemployment rose from six to twenty months. (Appendix Table 17) The number of persons who had been unemployed for a year or more was insignificant in 1929 and 1930, but by 1933, this group was a fourth of the total labor force and was as much as a sixth of the labor force even as late as 1936. The data available on the relation of age to duration of unemployment (Appendix Table 18) indicate that up to 1938, when a recession brought new layoffs affecting all age

18 There were 102,483 cases on the combined direct- and work-relief rolls of the County Relief Board of Philadelphia at the date of study in August 1936, approximately one-fourth of whom had been on relief rolls continuously for two or more years prior to that date.—Gladys L. Palmer and Janet H. Lewis, *The Long-Term Unemployed in Philadelphia in 1936*, Report No. P-8 (Philadelphia: WPA National Research Project in cooperation with Industrial Research Department, University of Pennsylvania, 1939).

groups, the average age of persons unemployed over one year steadily increased.

As the depression continued, each year's passing left a residual of persons in the group unemployed over a year who were not reabsorbed in the following year, and gradually there developed a "hard core" of long-term unemployed, whose chances of reabsorption diminished with each month or year of continued unemployment. One of the most distressing aspects of a long depression is the demoralizing effect on workers of months and years of unemployment. The loss of work-habits and skills has deteriorating effects on the individual and on all of his social relationships, and diminishes his chances of re-employment, since employers hesitate to hire someone who has been out of work for a long period of time.

Because of the importance of understanding the phenomenon of long-term unemployment, a special study was made of the group who might be considered the most immobile, namely, those persons who had been on relief rolls continuously for two or more years.[18] The characteristics of the chief wage earners in these families resembled those of other long-term unemployed in the city but differed from those of all other wage earners. They included relatively fewer women, many more Negroes, more unskilled workers, and they were older and less well educated than employed workers or than persons who had been out of a job for a relatively short period.

The importance of age and the absence of specialized work experience or skill as specific factors in the risks of long-term unemployment have been attested to in other studies in this country and abroad.[19] In Philadelphia, race was a factor in long-term unemployment independent of age for younger women and for men under 55, although its independence of the skill factor was not tested. Among

19 See *Men Without Work*—A report made to the Pilgrim Trust (London: Cambridge University Press, 1938), p. 24; Beveridge, *op. cit.*, pp. 65-72; Gladys L. Palmer and Katherine D. Wood, *Urban Workers on Relief*, WPA Research Monograph IV, Part I (Washington, 1936); R. G. D. Allen, "Unemployed Situation at Outbreak of the War," *Journal of the Royal Statistical Society*, Part II, 1940, pp. 206, 212; H. W. Singer, "The Process of Unemployment in the Depressed Areas, 1935-38," *Review of Economic Studies*, Vol. VI, No. 3 (June 1939), pp. 177-87; Leonard C. Marsh, *Canadians In and Out of Work* (Toronto: Oxford University Press, 1940), chap. XV; Colin Clark, *The Conditions of Economic Progress* (London: MacMillan & Co., Ltd., 1940), pp. 231-37, for a discussion of the relation of the general decline in the demand for unskilled labor to the supply of such labor.

urban workers on relief in 79 American cities in 1934, the association of such factors as level of education and length of previous experience with duration of unemployment was found to be significant only for those under 45 years of age.[20] The relationship of age and absence of skill to long-term unemployment reflects maladjustments between the structure of the labor force and that of the demand for labor, and these discrepancies were magnified by institutional forces, such as employers' hiring practices, particularly with respect to age.

These differences in the structure of labor supply and demand have a greater social import than merely to explain why some unemployed persons are out of work longer than others. In the words of one writer:

> Prolonged unemployment is a leveller which creates unskilled and unemployables as frequently as the reverse situation of lack of skill increases the risk of inferior employment and frequent lay-off, and below the white collar line it is often easier to fall than to rise.[21]

Unemployment is a process as well as a status, and, unfortunately, for all concerned, has self-perpetuating features, if prolonged. The dynamics of the process and associated characteristics of the persons affected therefore need continuing study if the essential problems are to be understood.

Family Employment and Unemployment

One might assume that, even with a large volume of unemployment for individual workers, a high proportion of multi-worker families in a city would spread the risks of unemployment among families, but this is not the case. Philadelphia is a city with a relatively high proportion of multi-worker families, but in a decade of annual sample surveys, it was found each year that there was a greater concentration of households with all workers unemployed than would be found if the unemployed worker-members had been distributed among households according to chance. Moreover, when single- and multi-worker families are compared, the workers in multi-worker households were unemployed in relatively greater numbers. This

20 Palmer and Wood, *op. cit.*, p. 94.
21 Marsh, *op. cit.*, p. 372.

is a significant finding in relation to the need for public aid, which is conditioned largely by family unemployment patterns and income needs.

In an earlier report, the explanation of this tendency to concentration of unemployment in multi-worker families is discussed at some length on the basis of evidence for several cities.[22] Briefly, the Philadelphia evidence indicates that the important employment characteristics of individuals, such as age, race, and usual occupation or industry are not randomly distributed in families and that families, as units, have characteristics that effect their unemployment risks. To state it differently, if there is a higher rate of unemployment for Negroes than for white workers, it stands to reason that Negro families will be unemployed in relatively greater numbers than white families. This was found to be the case in Philadelphia, where the rate of complete unemployment in families was 11 per cent for all multi-worker families in the sample in 1936, while it was 24 per cent for Negro families with more than one worker. Similarly, the rate of complete unemployment in multi-worker families where some members had usually been employed in the construction industry (28 per cent) was higher than the rate for families with members who had worked in other industry groups (9 per cent).[23] Although Philadelphia is not a specialized industrial center, in 1936 one third of the secondary workers in multi-worker families were usually employed in the same broad industry group as the primary wage earner. In multi-worker households reporting unemployment and in which the primary wage-earner and one or more other family members were usually employed in the same specific industry, it was found that from a fifth to a third of the latter lost their jobs in the same year as the household head.

The worker-composition of family units and the extent of customary employment in the same plant or industry therefore affect the unemployment risks of members of multi-worker families. It may also be noted that the workers in single-worker families are

22 Gladys L. Palmer, *The Significance of Employment Patterns in Households for Labor Market Analysis,* Special Report No. 8 (Philadelphia: Industrial Research Department, University of Pennsylvania, 1942). See also Don Humphrey, "Alleged Additional Workers in the Measurement of Unemployment," *Journal of Political Economy,* June 1940, pp. 413-14.

23 Unpublished data, 1936 Philadelphia sample survey.

predominantly males in the most employable age groups, while the workers in multi-worker families are predominantly secondary workers with a much wider range of employment characteristics. The rates of unemployment for workers in these two types of families would therefore be expected to differ. In summary, one may say that analysis of the family structure of the labor supply and of employment patterns, considering families as units, provides no evidence to support the "additional worker" theory, but has significance in planning programs for alleviating unemployment.

The Costs of Unemployment

Family or dependency responsibility and the incidence of unemployment in families are directly related to the problems of public aid. For the Philadelphia sample in May 1936, it was found that one-half of the families reporting unemployment were "known" to the Philadelphia County Relief Board and 40 per cent of them were "active" on relief rolls at that time. (They constituted 15 per cent of all households in the sample.) A comparison of relief and nonrelief households indicates that those in which some member was on relief rolls had fewer workers per family and that the average duration of unemployment for heads of such households was higher than for the heads of nonrelief households.[24]

In 1936, and again in 1939 when a subsequent check was made, over two-thirds of the households where all worker-members were unemployed (predominantly single-worker families) were on relief rolls.[25] The work status of the members of families considered as units, therefore, together with the dependency responsibility of the family head and the length of time he or she had been out of work were found to be closely associated with the receipt of public aid. In addition, insufficient or irregular income from certain types of employment in relation to dependency responsibilities or emergency situations, such as illness or accident, have periodically required some supplementation of income for a small group in the population. The number of persons in Philadelphia who received general assistance,

24 Palmer, *Employment and Unemployment in Philadelphia in 1936 and 1937*, Part I, pp. 11-14.

25 *Ibid.*, p. 12 and unpublished data from a small sample study made in cooperation with the Federal Work Projects Administration in 1939.

predominantly unemployment relief, during the depression years was a substantial proportion of the population and the direct costs of such aid were large.

The total economic and social costs of a decade of depression in a community are impossible to assess. In addition to the direct and indirect costs of general relief and other forms of public aid, there were extensive expenditures by private welfare agencies and informal aid given by relatives and friends. Many workers did not receive public or private aid, but lost their homes and other property or exhausted the savings of a lifetime. The community's standard of living was reduced as income dropped, marriage and birth rates declined, and a variety of indicators of social disorganization testified to the deteriorating effects of the depression on the social life of the community.

Perhaps the losses to the labor force were the most important to the economy because they affected future productive capacity. The strain of subsistence living affected the health and morale of the population. There was a substantial loss of skill and work-habits on the part of experienced workers while inexperienced workers failed to secure an opportunity to learn work-habits or acquire experience. Few apprentices to the skilled crafts were trained during these years and when the demand for labor increased rapidly at the time of our entrance into World War II, labor shortages were more acute by reason of the absence of such training in the previous decade. The personnel manager of a large munitions plant in the city commented on the fact that he had never fully realized the effects of the depression until he began to review hundreds of work records on applications for war jobs and found capable men with years of no work or little or no experience worth recording.

By the end of the thirties, unemployment had become "the principal practical problem of our generation."[26] A decade of depression had convinced the public that relief was "not enough" and that reducing frictions in the labor market, desirable as that might be, was not an adequate program when the total demand for labor was insufficient to employ the labor force for years on end. Some new

[26] Arthur F. Burns, *Economic Research and the Keynesian Thinking of Our Time*, Twenty-fifth Annual Report (New York: National Bureau of Economic Research, 1946), p. 4.

approach to the problem was necessary. With the advent of World War II, unprecedented government expenditures for military requirements created an abnormally heavy demand for labor; employment increased rapidly and the "hard core" of long-term unemployment melted away; new recruits had to be brought into the civilian labor force to staff war industries or to replace persons drawn into the military services. The war developments are discussed in some detail in the next chapter, but it may be noted here that they intensified interest in public policies directed to the maintenance of stable and high levels of employment as a social responsibility. Numerous governments, including our own, have recently adopted, in one form or another, a statement of policy accepting such responsibility,[27] and future years will undoubtedly see experiments designed to secure a new approach to the problems of large-scale unemployment.

---

[27] *Public Law No. 304,* 79th Cong., 2nd Sess. (February 20, 1946), "Employment Act of 1946."

Chapter VI

The Effects of War Prosperity on the Labor Market

THE DEFENSE and war production programs reversed most of the trends of the previous decade in Philadelphia, as elsewhere in the nation, and wrought spectacular changes in the labor market. As the demand for labor increased, unemployment declined rapidly. From March 1940 to December 1941, Philadelphia's rate of unemployment fell from about one fifth of the labor force to six per cent. Concomitantly, the number of Philadelphia residents employed in industry and the armed forces rose to exceed any level previously recorded, and the number of job openings filed with the United States Employment Service offices in Philadelphia quadrupled between mid-1940 and the end of 1941.

After Pearl Harbor, the demand for industrial labor continued at a high level and there was an increase in the number of men required in military service. Although the total labor force of the city (including persons serving in the armed forces) continued to expand until a peak was reached in the spring of 1945, the civilian labor force declined. The peak of munitions employment was reached in the fall of 1943 and levelled off after that, as increasing numbers entered military service. A variety of new recruits were attracted to the labor market during this period: young people left school to go to work if not to enter military service; retired persons returned to the labor market; and a substantial number of housewives secured employment. Of equal importance was the fact that migration from other communities to the Philadelphia area added substantial numbers to the local labor supply.

Workers in munitions factories were recruited from a wide range of industries. Although most of the munitions work in the area required male employees because of the predominance of shipbuilding and heavy ordnance, women replaced men leaving other jobs and their numbers increased steadily, even in munitions factories. The proportion of women to the total employed in the city increased from 31 per cent in 1940 to 38 per cent in 1944 and 1945. In fact, more women were added to the city's labor force between 1940 and 1945 than over the three decades from 1910 to 1940.

Shortages of skilled labor developed in such occupations as machinists and toolmakers at an early stage in the defense program. Labor shortages became more general as the war continued, although Philadelphia was not officially classified as a "shortage area" by the War Manpower Commission until the summer of 1944. During 1943, an employment stabilization plan was in effect in the local labor-market area and a limited program of hiring quotas and priority referrals was introduced by the War Manpower Commission early in 1944. This program was made more stringent in July 1944, when employment ceilings and controlled referrals to all jobs in the area were introduced in the interest of assuring a labor supply to essential war industries.

Tightening of the labor market relaxed the hiring specifications of employers even before labor-market controls were officially introduced. Inexperienced workers could secure jobs at relatively high rates of pay without difficulty. Older workers now found excellent job opportunities. Negroes were accepted for many types of jobs hitherto closed to them. Women not only became an increasingly important source of additional labor supply, but entered jobs that had previously employed only men. As the market became more stringent, skill was at a premium and skilled jobs were broken down into less skilled operations. Many workers were upgraded in rates of pay or degree of responsibility during the war, and extensive training programs were instituted to staff essential industries.

Most of the munitions plants in the area had been in operation prior to the war and had a nucleus of experienced workers to maintain production. Expansion was, therefore, very rapid. By November 1943, more Philadelphia residents were employed in the munitions industries alone than in all manufacturing in March 1940. The index of factory employment in the local area, based on the prewar year of 1939, rose by more than half and the index of factory payrolls almost doubled between 1940 and 1944.

As in other areas, the conclusion of the war brought contraction of industrial activity, reconversion to peacetime pursuits, and the return of a large proportion of the men serving in the armed forces. Despite substantial layoffs after V-J day, however, the levels of civilian employment in 1947 and 1948 were higher than in May 1945. Although some persons retired from the labor market after losing jobs in war industries or after the return of the usual wage earner from the armed forces, the total labor force of the Philadelphia Metropolitan Area in the postwar years was markedly higher than in March 1940, and employment, here as elsewhere, was at a record level for peacetime conditions. Unemployment rates during the postwar years were higher in this and other metropolitan centers than in the nation, but were low compared with 1940 and the preceding decade.

This brief summary of the labor-market changes that took place during the war and reconversion periods affords a background for the more detailed analysis that follows. Emphasis is placed on changes in the volume and nature of labor-market transactions and on employment trends and labor mobility in the period since 1940. A comparison of local and national trends highlights the differential impact of the spectacular changes that occurred during the war and postwar years throughout the nation.

War Expansion

Many private plants, as well as the Government establishments located in the Philadelphia area, received defense contracts in 1940 and 1941, particularly in shipbuilding and heavy armament, and, shortly after Pearl Harbor, most of the metal products plants in the area converted to the production of munitions. The labor shortages of the early war years occurred in the skilled occupations in these industries, such as toolmakers, machinists, instrument makers, loftsmen, shipfitters, and coppersmiths. As production got under way, however, labor requirements were modified to utilize less skilled workers under the supervision of craftsmen through special training programs or reorganization of the work. The number of apprentice training programs and of apprentices also increased. Interstate recruiting by the United States Employment Service and by plants and the voluntary migration of workers helped to reduce local shortages in these occupations.

During 1942, war contracts spread to textile, apparel, leather, chemical, and other industries. Subcontracting of parts manufacture resulted in a wider spread of war work and led to a mushroom growth of "cellar industrialists" who converted garages and their own small machine shops to the production of munitions parts. Military supplies of infinite variety began to roll off the production lines. The national restriction of materials to war use and subsequent decline of affected operations caused some "conversion unemployment," but it was of short duration. Unemployed workers secured jobs quickly and voluntary shifts of workers from less essential to more essential jobs proceeded apace. By the summer and fall of 1943, the "manpower crisis" had drawn the attention of newspaper editorials and headlines; it led to more extensive training and recruiting programs and, eventually, to the introduction of manpower controls.

Chart 6 and Appendix Table 19 provide annual data on various types of labor-market activity in the years following World War I, using 1947-1949 as a base for indexes. Levels of the use of help-wanted advertising and the public employment service in World War II and the postwar years reflect labor shortages in the forties as compared with the thirties, but also reflect increased use of these hiring channels as compared with levels in the twenties. On the other hand, employment certificates issued to minors were a legal requirement enforced throughout the period. The latter index portrays levels on a more comparable basis over all the years covered, despite a change in the age level for compulsory education. The numbers of jobs held by minors is sensitive to variations in business conditions. The lesson of this chart is that it takes a relatively large volume of recruiting and hiring to keep jobs filled in a city in periods of rapidly expanding employment.

Some of the lessons of World War I experience were guides to manpower controls in World War II. Competitive bidding for workers on the part of industry during World War I, in a market with no wage or price controls, led to extensive "pirating" of labor,

CHART 6—Selected Labor-Market Indicators, Philadelphia, 1921-1953

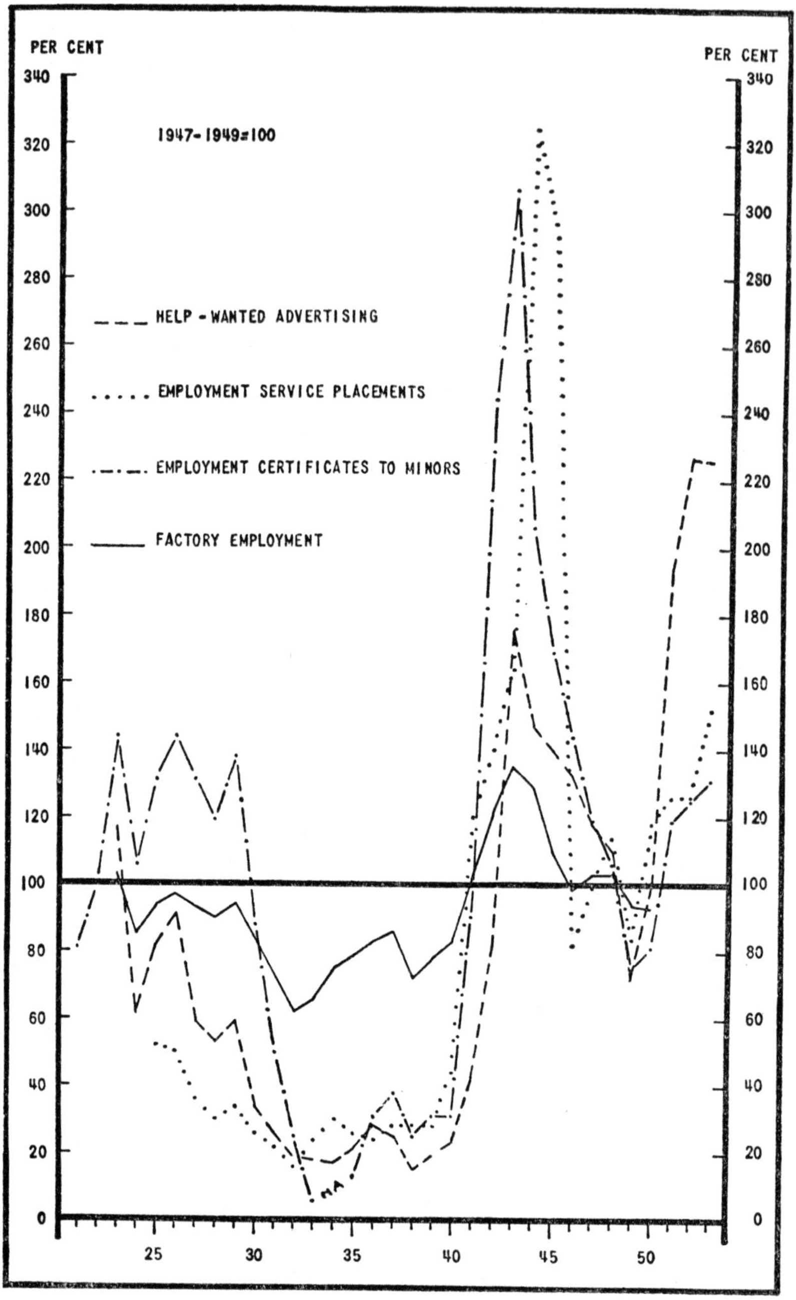

SOURCE: Appendix table 19

excessively high labor turnover, and disorganized production schedules. A shortage of unskilled labor developed in the early stages of World War I and, in 1918, employers were asked to refrain from recruiting unskilled labor except through the United States Employment Service, and the use of help-wanted advertising was controlled or prohibited. In World War II, it was recognized that all recruiting resources would be needed if production demands were to be met and there were no restrictions on recruiting, although hirings for war jobs as a result of help-wanted advertising or direct recruiting were channeled through the Employment Service offices. The institution of wage-controls and of the so-called "job-freeze" reduced labor turnover among employees on the job. In the latter case, workers were not permitted to transfer from one war plant to another without a certificate of release from the Employment Service. After it became clear that voluntary recruiting for war jobs would not suffice to meet the demand, steps were taken to force transfers from less essential to more essential industries by the national order to men of draft age "to get a war job or a rifle."[1]

Numerous community activities assisted in stretching the available labor supply to meet war demands. Early in 1943, it was estimated that 183,000 persons had been specially trained for war work in the Philadelphia area.[2] Schools modified schedules to permit longer holiday periods for temporary employment of students. Combined school-and-work programs were initiated to give school credit for part-time employment experience by persons just below the legal age for full-time employment. Community facilities were developed to make it easier for women with family responsibilities to work long hours. Transportation and housing facilities were improved for war workers. Prison labor was diverted to war contract work. Recruiting campaigns drew more housewives and debutantes into war jobs and attracted migrants from other areas. By the spring of 1944, more than three out of every five persons, 14 years of age or over, in the city were in the civilian labor force or the armed services.

The introduction of the 48-hour week, experimentation with split shifts for part-time workers, and the setting of employment "ceilings" in 1943 reduced manpower requirements to a limited extent.

1 *The Philadelphia Record,* February 3, 1943.
2 *Ibid.*, April 26, 1943.

Despite these developments, the bottom of the manpower "barrel" had been scraped by the summer of 1944, and the Philadalphia area was declared a general labor-shortage area to which no further war contracts could be awarded. As the city's manpower situation had tightened, new "bottlenecks" had appeared. By the fall of 1943, it was difficult to secure men for unskilled jobs, particularly for heavy work in boiler shops and foundries, because of the preference of workers for machine-operating jobs.[3] Wages and working conditions were partially responsible for this type of shortage.

Early in 1945, the priority classifications for referring workers to jobs were reorganized in favor of 41 plants where the production of "top urgency" combat items was lagging because of manpower shortages.[4] Plans were developed for employer and union cooperation in transferring 11,000 workers from less essential industries to war plants. Transfer operations under this plan had just gotten under way[5] when the war in Europe ended. Local manpower controls were then relaxed and the area was reclassified as a locality in which any labor shortages that existed did not hamper national war production. By the end of the summer of 1945, the war in the Pacific was over and the process of demobilization had begun.

Through June 1945, the Philadelphia-Camden Industrial Area had received war contracts to the value of over eight billion dollars, of which over ninety per cent were supply contracts. Six per cent of this total went into the construction of industrial facilities and less than two per cent into military installations.[6] The cancellation of contracts after the close of the war was estimated to affect over 6,000 plants in the area.[7]

The magnitude of wartime personnel recruiting and placement problems is evidenced in the fact that half of all Philadelphia wage and salary workers who were at work in May 1944 had started with their employers after Pearl Harbor.[8] At no time since World War I

3 *Ibid.*, September 6, 1943.

4 *Ibid.*, January 13, 16, 17, 1945.

5 Approximately 250 candy, hat, and soda factory workers had been transferred under this plan.—*Ibid.*, May 29, 1945.

6 *Tax and Facts Bulletin* (Philadelphia Chamber of Commerce), April 8, 1946.

7 *The Philadelphia Inquirer*, June 14, 1944.

8 Gladys L. Palmer, *The Philadelphia Labor Market in 1944*, Research Report No. 8 (Philadelphia: Industrial Research Department, University of Pennsylvania, 1942), p. 18.

had the proportion of short-service workers in the city's labor force been so high. By contrast, the average length of service of all Philadelphia workers (including self-employed persons) was 8.3 years for men and 4.8 for women in 1938.[9]

Between 1940 and 1945, substantial proportions of children left school to go to work and retired persons re-entered the labor market both in Philadelphia and in the United States. (Appendix Table 20) In the nation, there was a ten per cent decline in the number of women whose major activity was reported as housework, but the numbers of women who were nonworkers increased in the city. In this five-year period the city gained relatively twice as much population as the nation and in-migration contributed more workers to the city's labor force than were added through increased rates of labor-force participation of nonmigrants.[10] Manufacturing and government activities made spectacular gains in employment during the war, both locally and nationally, and these gains were frequently accomplished at the expense of other industries.

A measure of the wartime shifts made by individual workers was obtained through a survey of what persons who were employed in the spring of 1944 had been doing the week before Pearl Harbor. (Appendix Table 21)[11] The over-all stability of the labor force is indicated in the fact that four out of every five workers in both the nation and the city in 1944 had been in the labor force in December 1941, and three out of five were employed in the same broad industry group at both dates. Fifteen per cent of the nation's workers and 17 per cent of the city's workers who were employed at both dates were attached to a different major industry group in 1944. One out of every five workers in the nation's workshops in 1944 had been out of the labor market in December 1941 as compared with 18 per cent of local workers. A majority of the latter group in both instances had been in school or engaged in keeping house at the time of Pearl Harbor. Munitions factories, whether local or national, had drawn

9 Gladys L. Palmer, *Employment and Unemployment in Philadelphia, July August, 1938*, Special Report No. 7 (Philadelphia: Industrial Research Department, University of Pennsylvania, 1939), p. 16.

10 The estimated labor force in 1944 had 89,000 more workers than would have been expected had 1940 rates of labor-force participation prevailed; and between 1940 and 1944, an estimated 63,000 workers had migrated to Philadelphia.—Palmer, *The Philadelphia Labor Market in 1944*, pp. 4, 30.

11 Based on unpublished tabulations from the sources listed in Appendix Table 21.

more than half of their employees from other industry groups or from persons not previously employed.

The seven industry groups used in compiling Table 6 are very broad and understate the amount and kind of changes that took place during the war, for some workers changed jobs more than once between the two dates and, within a broad industry group, there was shifting between employers. In Philadelphia, for example, approximately a fifth of the workers who were employed in the same broad industry group on both dates had changed employers.

Table 6

NET GAINS OR LOSSES[a] TO EMPLOYMENT BY REASON OF INDUSTRY SHIFTS PHILADELPHIA AND THE UNITED STATES 1941-1944[b]

Industry group	Philadelphia		United States	
	Net gains or losses (in 000's)	Per cent of December 1941 employment	Net gains or losses (in 000's)	Per cent of December 1941 employment
Manufacturing	+51	+18.9	+2,205	+19.5
Munitions	+65	+52.4	+2,596	+48.4
Other manufacturing	−14	− 9.6	− 391	− 4.9
Transportation, communications, utilities	+ 2	+ 4.8	+ 245	+ 7.4
Trade	−20	−14.7	− 919	−13.8
Finance, business, professional services	−11	−13.1	− 208	− 4.5
Personal services	−15	−24.6	− 431	−13.6
Other nonmanufacturing	− 7	− 9.2	− 819	− 7.4

Source: Data for Philadelphia from unpublished tabulations of survey made by the Industrial Research Department in cooperation with the Bureau of the Census for May 1944; data for the United States from Bureau of the Census, *Current Population Reports*, Series P-50, No. 1, Table A, and unpublished tabulations.

[a] Net gains or losses refer to the balance between accessions to and separations from an industry group by workers employed at both dates.

[b] The data cover changes from December 1941 to March 1944 for the United States and to May 1944 for Philadelphia.

As might be expected, gains to the munitions manufacturing industries accounted for a substantial number of the industry-group shifts made by workers who were employed both at the time of Pearl Harbor and in the spring of 1944. (Table 6) Except for these industries and the group including transportation, communications, and utilities, all other industry groups registered net losses by reason of the industry shifts of workers employed at both dates. The extent of shifting out of the service industries and out of manufacturing other than munitions was relatively greater in Philadelphia than in the nation. This evidence would appear to support the view that Philadelphians were equally if not more mobile than the average worker in the nation, in terms of wartime shifts.

There is also evidence of mobility between major occupational groups both nationally and locally during this period. Movement from lower to higher levels of major occupational groups was more pronounced for women than for men and for Negroes than for white workers in Philadelphia, partly as a result of their starting from lower levels than male white workers. Within major occupational groups, collateral evidence indicates a considerable upgrading for rate of pay or job assignment for men as well as women and for white as well as Negro workers. Employment, like unemployment, is a process as well as a status, and opportunities for promotion and new experience during the war resulted in a more flexible and better trained labor force in the community as a whole.

As a result of withdrawals to military service and of shifts in the employment of civilians, declines in the professional group, for both men and women, and in male clerical and service work took place at a relatively higher rate locally than nationally.[11] On the other hand, operatives and laborers of both sexes increased more rapidly in Philadelphia than in the United States. These changes reflected shifts that were necessitated by the drafting of men for military service, and, to some extent, the drift of workers from white-collar to manual occupations. A preference for white-collar work that had characterized the two preceding decades may have disappeared during World War II, as factory wage rates rose and the opportunities for higher earnings and promotions increased. In fact, what might appear to be a downgrading in level of skill as a result of shifts of some workers from service to laborers' jobs or from clerical to factory jobs may well have netted higher earnings and more opportunity for advancement to individuals.

Demobilization and Reconversion

Cutbacks in munitions orders toward the end of the war brought layoffs, reductions in earnings, and shifts from munitions to other industries. In January 1946, for example, there were only 200 employees left in a shipyard in the Delaware River Basin that had had a peak employment of 9,600 in 1943.[12] A survey of the experience of a sample of persons on the shipyard payroll in 1945 indicated that a fourth were unemployed in January 1946, about half had secured other jobs, and the remaining fourth had left the area or retired from the labor market. Less than half of those employed in 1946 were working at their prewar occupations. The earnings of the workers while at the shipyard had been higher than prewar earnings and also higher than earnings in jobs secured after the layoffs. The extent of job shifting during the war is reflected in the fact that almost all of the workers in this shipyard had held two or more jobs and two-thirds had held from four to nine jobs, each, in the five years between January 1941 and January 1946.

The experience of the shipyard workers illustrates the character of job shifting that occurred on a much broader scale during and after the war in munitions industries throughout the area and nation. A local newspaper poll in January 1946 found that one out of every eight men and one out of every 20 women in the city had changed jobs between the end of the war and that date.[13] The shifts of most women had resulted from the closing of war plants, although only one-third of the men who changed jobs attributed this action to shutdowns. As in other periods of rapid employment changes, voluntary as well as involuntary shifts had occurred. Somewhat later in the year of 1946, it was found that for the nation as a whole, one out of every eight workers (both men and women) employed in civilian jobs just before V-J Day had jobs in another industry group twelve months later.[14] During the same year, one out of every nine persons employed in both August 1945 and August 1946 had changed from one major occupational group to another.[15] Even in the early reconversion years, the expansion of employment opportunity in industries that had been restricted during the war tended to offset a decline in employment in war industries. It should be noted again that

---

12 *Wartime Shipbuilding Workers of Wilmington, Delaware,* U. S. Bureau of Labor Statistics, Work and Wage Experience Studies, Report No. 4 (June 1946), p. 3.

13 "The Bulletin Poll," *The Evening Bulletin* (Philadelphia), January 4, 1946.

14 U. S. Bureau of the Census, *Current Population Reports,* Series P-50 (July 1947), No. 1, p. 1.

15 *Ibid.,* p. 2.

this offset was aided by the return to school of some young people who had left for war jobs or military service and by the retirement of some persons from the labor market after V-J Day.[16]

Reconversion of the local economy to peacetime pursuits was comparatively less difficult in the Philadelphia area than in many other communities. This was because war demands had been met for the most part by expansion of existing facilities. A small proportion of total Government expenditures in this as in other established industrial areas was allocated to the building of new facilities. Also, the products made in the area were readily converted to peacetime uses. Shipbuilding was an exception in the sense that the demand for ships in peacetime has never equalled the demand during a war, although shipyards in the Delaware Basin have always produced vessels for the merchant marine as well as for the Navy. The iron and steel products, heavy machinery, machine parts, and electrical equipment, characteristic of this area's economy, were diverted to other uses after the war. Production in the nondurable goods industries that had been restricted by material shortages during the war increased substantially after the war ended. Trade and service industries that had been handicapped by labor shortages or manpower restrictions during the war expanded to meet a heavy demand for consumers' goods and services, while factory employment declined.

The peak of manufacturing employment in the city and area had been reached in 1943 (Appendix Table 5), and leveled off or declined slightly after that period. The most drastic expansion and decline occurred in the shipbuilding and aircraft industries that dominated the transportation equipment group. Despite the layoffs after the close of the war in the Pacific area, employment levels in the metal-products industries in 1946 were approximately twice as high as in 1939, and the 1946 employment levels in nondurable goods industries were back to prewar levels or above, except in the case of textile products, in which both conversion and reconversion had created special problems. The conversion of most of the specialized weaving equipment of the mills in this area to the manufacture of heavy duck and other war materials wore out the equipment, and, as a result, reconversion was delayed in these industries.

16 Between August 1945 and August 1946, an estimated four million workers left the national labor force.—*Monthly Labor Review,* November 1940, p. 670.

No estimates of the numbers of persons affected by the closing of war facilities or cancellation of war contracts are available. However, average annual employment in the metal-products industries (exclusive of Government establishments) in the five-county area was 86,000 lower in 1946 than in 1943 (Appendix Table 5), and workers in other industries were also affected by contract cancellations. Postwar factory layoffs began to have a noticeable effect on the number of persons receiving unemployment compensation by September 1945. The weekly average of slightly over 1,000 compensable claims in Philadelphia county in July and August of 1945 increased to 15,000 by the end of September and to 28,000 in April 1946. Returning veterans, who were entitled to Servicemen's Readjustment Allowances, applied for SRA pay orders in increasing numbers after the end of the war. The weekly average of such pay orders increased from approximately 300 in August 1945 to 42,000 in April 1946. Postwar peaks of compensable unemployment claims and SRA pay orders combined were reached in the years 1946 and 1949. (Appendix Table 19)

The reabsorption of returning veterans into the civilian economy after the close of the war was a major focus of attention during 1946. The seniority and "superseniority" rights of veterans to jobs displaced large numbers of workers, who, in turn, displaced others with less tenure. The year 1946 was therefore characterized by a large-scale shuffling around in jobs as well as by the closing of war facilities, layoffs, and some migration from the city. In many ways, this year was like 1941: levels of activity were almost the same, and the outlook held many uncertainties for both business and labor. Higher rates of unemployment, labor turnover, and strike activity reflected the impact of insecurity on workers. By 1947, however, employment had turned upward, unemployment had leveled off, and the local economy had all of the attributes of prosperity. High levels of economic activity persisted through 1948, but by the end of that year there were increasing uncertainties in the business situation. Large-scale inventory reductions between the end of 1948 and the third quarter of 1949 initiated a business recession. During this period, unemployment in the Philadelphia labor market rose from an estimated level of 78,000 in July 1948 to 124,000 in June 1949 and

135,000 in February 1950.[17] The decade as a whole, however, had been one of relatively high levels of employment.

The rate of unemployment in Philadelphia dropped from 20 per cent of the labor force in 1940 to 2 and 3 per cent during World War II and rose to 7 per cent in 1946, 1947, and 1950. (Appendix Table 15) It was probably higher in 1949, but data are not available to provide comparable estimates. Despite a remarkably low level of unemployment during the decade, its incidence among various groups of workers paralleled some of the experience in the thirties. The rate of unemployment for nonwhite workers was usually double or slightly more than double that for white workers. In general, the youngest and oldest members of the city's labor force, especially those from 14 to 24 years of age, had higher rates of unemployment than workers in the intermediate age groups. Relatively high sampling variance for the unemployed counts makes it difficult to draw conclusions, but there is some evidence to indicate that the unemployment rates for women were higher than those for men during World War II, but that men had higher rates than women in 1940 and from 1946 to 1950. To the extent that unemployment rates during World War II were affected by a high rate of labor-force turnover among women, this finding might be expected. High job and/or labor-force turnover among young workers may account for their rates of unemployment during this relatively prosperous decade. But the difference between white and nonwhite workers reflects traditional hiring practices, the short tenure of service and laboring jobs frequently held by Negroes, and also the fact that many of them have recently migrated from the rural South and lack the industrial skills required in a diversified labor market. It may be noted that the city of Philadelphia has had since 1948 a Fair Employment Practice Ordinance that prohibits discrimination in employment on racial or religious grounds.

Mobility Patterns over the Decade, 1940 1950

The defense and war production needs of the forties had a permanent effect on the employment structure of both the city and the nation. In occupational terms, Philadelphia's employment in

---

17 Bimonthly reports of the Philadelphia District Office of the Pennsylvania State Employment Service.

managerial and clerical occupations and in the skilled crafts gained at higher rates than total employment between 1940 and 1950. In the nation, all major occupational groups except service workers and laborers gained at a higher rate than total employment.[18] National industrial trends between 1940 and 1950 varied somewhat from those in the city. National gains were relatively high in three of the industries that expanded at a high rate in Philadelphia: construction, public administration, and transportation and utilities. However, national manufacturing and trade gained at higher than local rates. Employment in the extractive industries declined nationally and in the personal service industries, both locally and nationally. (Appendix Table 20) Despite substantial wartime gains in manufacturing in Philadelphia, net gains over the decade were less than half as high as in the nation.

Over the decade as a whole, the national civilian labor force gained at about the same rate as the population 14 years of age and over, but the Philadelphia labor force remained almost stationary in size. Local employment levels were higher, and unemployment levels lower, in 1950 than in 1940, but employment gains were relatively higher in the nation than in the city. In general, local trends in the various categories of nonworkers paralleled those in the nation. (Appendix Table 20) A striking trend in both cases was a substantial decline in the school population. The major differences in the experience of the nation and the city between 1940 and 1950 occurred in relative employment levels and structural changes in employment.

The evidence presented in various sections of this chapter and supplementary data from the 1951 work-history study indicate that employment expanded in certain industries both through accessions to employment and interindustry transfers of experienced workers. The nature of the goods and services produced in an industry, however, does not set up the same kind of barriers to labor mobility that flow from the job requirements at various levels of skill.[19] Occupational differentials in mobility appear to be more marked than indus-

---

18 Rates of increase for Philadelphia were computed from *1950 Census of Population, Preliminary Reports,* PC-5, No. 36, Table 11, and for the United States from *1950 Census of Population, General Characteristics,* Vol. II, part 1, p. 102.

19 Gladys L. Palmer, *Labor Mobility in Six Cities* (New York: Social Science Research Council, 1954), pp. 92-93, 127-28, 129-31.

trial differentials. For that reason, attention is drawn to the occupational patterns in work attachments in 1940 and 1950 and the types of employer shifts made by persons who were 25 years of age and over and had worked one month or more in 1950.

For both sexes combined, as many workers made intergroup occupational shifts between 1940 and 1950 as entered employment from another labor-force status in 1940. Moreover, the numbers making occupational changes were substantially higher than the number of migrants to the city after 1940. Migrants added relatively large numbers to the 1940 employment of workers in professional, managerial, and service occupations. Accessions to employment from another status were relatively more important in service and clerical occupations and for operatives than for other types of occupations. On the other hand, shifts from other occupational groups made relatively large contributions to 1940 levels of employment in managerial occupations and the skilled crafts over the decade. (Table 7) Despite these changes in status or type of work, 72 per cent of all nonmigrants who were employed at both dates were in the same occupational group in 1950 as in 1940 and this proportion was even higher in professional, managerial, and service occupations. This proportion was lowest for sales workers, a group that experienced a relatively high proportion of outward shifts between 1940 and 1950.

Professional occupations thus expanded primarily through the training of new workers and in-migration. In Philadelphia there were twice as many new accessions as shifts from other groups and migration also added to the numbers in this group. Managerial occupations expanded primarily through transfers from other occupational groups. Clerical occupations, usually more readily entered and left than are others, required an unusual proportion of new workers in this decade, because of high labor-force turnover among women and outward shifts by men. The skilled crafts expanded largely through shifts of experienced workers from other groups, while operatives gained primarily through accessions to the labor force. Service occupations lost relatively few workers and gained through accessions and migration. Laborers gained slightly more than they lost, but the rate of loss to other groups was substantial. These differences in the relative importance of intergroup occupational shifts from, and of new accessions to, various levels of skill over a decade

Table 7

Effect of Intergroup Shifts and Accessions to Employment Philadelphia, 1940-1950

Occupational group	Intergroup shifts and accessions to employment, 1940-1950, for workers 25 years of age or over in 1951						
	Nonmigrants					Migrants employed in [a] 1950	Total 25+ employed in 1950 by 1950 distribution[b]
	Persons 14+ employed in Jan. 1940 by 1940 distribution	Employed in same group in 1950	Added from other groups by 1950	Lost to other groups by 1950	Accessions from other status by 1950[a]		
				Numbers in Thousands			
All occupations	507	366	141	-141	141	92	740
Professional workers	35	30	5	- 5	10	8	53
Managerial workers	46	38	29	- 8	6	12	85
Clerical workers	64	43	16	- 21	25	9	93
Sales workers	37	20	9	- 17	11	5	45
Craftsmen	85	62	26	- 23	12	12	112
Operatives	144	103	34	- 41	47	23	207
Service workers	56	45	14	- 11	24	16	99
Laborers	40	25	8	- 15	6	7	46
				Per cent of 1940			
All occupations	100	72	28	- 28	28	18	146
Professional workers	100	86	14	- 14	28	23	151
Managerial workers	100	83	63	- 17	13	26	185
Clerical workers	100	67	25	- 33	39	14	145
Sales workers	100	54	24	- 46	30	14	122
Craftsmen	100	73	31	- 27	14	14	132
Operatives	100	72	24	- 28	32	16	144
Service workers	100	80	25	- 20	43	29	177
Laborers	100	63	20	- 37	15	17	115

Source: Unpublished data from the Survey of Patterns and Factors in Labor Mobility, 1940-1950, which was summarized in Gladys L. Palmer, *Labor Mobility in Six Cities* (New York: Social Science Research Council, 1954).

[a] Includes persons in the Armed Forces, unemployed, or not in the labor force in 1940.

[b] The occupation held in 1950 refers to the occupation of longest job during the year.

give clues to the recruitment and training problems in a labor market during a period of rapid changes in employment.

Of the estimated 742,000 Philadelphia workers studied by a work-history sample survey in 1951, 43 per cent had worked for only one employer during the decade and 57 per cent had had more than one employer. Some 400,000 workers made 880,000 employer shifts[20] during the decade. Over half of this movement involved the simultaneous change of employer, occupation, and industry[21] and next in importance were changes of employer and industry. Women more frequently changed employer without changing occupation or industry than men. (Chart 7, Appendix Table 22) Professional workers, craftsmen, and women operatives and managers were also more likely than other workers to have made changes of employer only. Women in clerical occupations made a relatively high proportion of shifts involving changes of employer and industry or of employer, occupation, and industry, while the majority of male clerical workers made the latter type of shift. Sales workers and male operatives made a relatively large number of combined shifts, although service workers reported the highest proportions of such shifts. The job changes of male laborers followed the general patterns for men, except for a higher proportion of shifts of employer unaccompanied by other changes.

About three-fourths of the job separations of Philadelphia workers during the decade from 1940 to 1950 were voluntary, but supplementary evidence indicates that the same shift patterns were followed whether or not the job separations had been caused by layoffs. Moreover, there were no substantial differences in these mobility patterns in six cities studied simultaneously, despite intercity variations in rates of job mobility. Philadelphia workers were the least mobile of any in the six cities studied in terms of the average number of changes of status, job, or employer that occurred per worker between 1940 and 1950, or in the proportion of workers affected by such changes,[22] but the kinds of shifts they made paralleled those in other cities.

---

20 The count of employer shifts is an understatement because it excludes the records of persons who worked in casual jobs throughout the decade and because the records for casual jobs of other workers were condensed.

21 Changes of occupation and industry were so counted if they involved the application of a different code among 269 occupation items and 146 industry items

If one compares the patterns of job changes made by male factory workers from 1940 to 1950 with those made by men in selected factory occupations (adjusted for age coverage) from 1925 to 1936, some noteworthy differences are found. (Appendix Table 23) In each case, there was a five-year period of relatively high peacetime employment levels (1926-1930, 1945-1949) and a five-year period characterized by major interruption to work experience. In the earlier study, large-scale unemployment interrupted usual patterns of work experience and in the later study, service in the Armed Forces. A basic difference in the coverage of the two studies flows from the fact that the group studied in 1936 was composed almost exclusively of craftsmen and operatives, the craftsmen constituting almost half of men 25 years of age or over at the date of study. In the group studied in 1951, all grades of skill were included and craftsmen constituted only 13 per cent of the total.

Although more job separations per worker were reported for 1940 to 1949 than for 1925 to 1936, there were more job changes and employer shifts in the earlier decade. While the general contours of the distribution of employer shifts by type was the same in both decades, shifts of employer only were relatively more numerous in the earlier, and combinations of shifts in the later, period. It is not known whether these differences reflect a change in the strength of factory workers' attachments to specific occupations or types of work over the decades or whether the special circumstances of each decade influenced the pattern. The difference does not reflect a predominance of craftsmen in the earlier study.[23] If anything, the number of employer shifts that involved a change of occupation or industry is somewhat overstated in the earlier as compared with the later study, because of a mechanical difference in coding occupational and industrial changes (see footnotes to Appendix Table 23).

---

in the classifications of the U. S. Bureau of the Census.

22 Palmer, *Labor Mobility in Six Cities*, pp. 52, 114.

23 If one excludes from consideration the records of machinists and toolmakers (except for apprentices), who constituted 40 per cent of the total, the proportion of craftsmen in the study made in 1936 is the same as for the group studied in 1951. The average numbers of job separations and job and employer shifts per worker for the remainder is higher. The resulting distribution of type of employer shifts is: employer only, 39 per cent; employer and occupation, 6 per cent; employer and industry, 10 per cent; and employer, occupation, and industry, 45 per cent.

CHART 7—Type of Employer Shift, 1940-1949, by Workers' Occupational Group in 1950 and Sex, Philadelphia

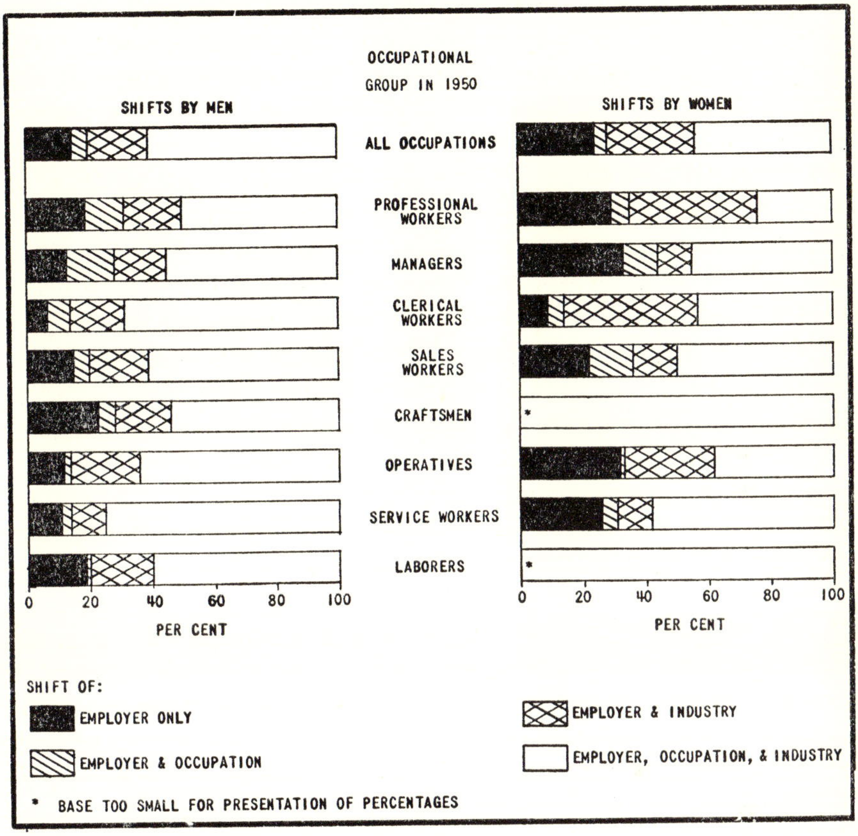

SOURCE: Appendix table 22

Moreover, there appear to have been more changes of occupational assignment with the same employer in the earlier than in the later period, although one might have assumed that the chances for a change of occupational assignment with the same employer would have been greater in the forties than in the earlier period. A final answer to these questions awaits further research, but patterns of labor-market behavior appear to have changed over time and such changes may have implications for vocational guidance and personnel programs as well as for knowledge of factors in the degree and character of mobility in a city's labor force.

War and Postwar Experience in the Longer-Term Setting

Recent labor-market developments in Philadelphia and other cities emphasize the ability of diversified economies to meet a wide range of production needs through the flexibility in size, composition, and experience of their labor forces. The normal labor force of this city and area is now better trained and inherently more mobile because a substantial number of its workers shifted jobs and acquired new skills or experience during the war. Moreover, a large part of the adult population is prepared to undertake productive work when emergencies arise because a larger proportion has had work experience. These developments will enhance future labor resources.

Higher levels of wage rates and earnings in the war and postwar years also had important effects on community life. Their most obvious effect was to raise standards of living above the straightened circumstances of the preceding decade. Backlogs of savings and higher income levels, together with programs of special aid to veterans, had the additional effect of enabling persons to take a chance on changing jobs, starting a new business, or moving to a different area. The mobility of labor requires some capital or security for the risk involved in making the changes. Although by no means conclusive, recent experience suggests that, in an old industrial center, the mobility of labor is accelerated by the "pulls" of opportunity rather than by the "pushes" of adversity.

The training of young persons benefited from war and postwar developments. Income supplements for the education of veterans swelled the ranks of students in schools and colleges. While some students left school for work during World War II before completion of scheduled courses and did not return, their numbers were more than offset by those who attended school in the postwar period and might not otherwise have been able to take training.

There have also been gains to the local economy that may have permanent effects on its industrial characteristics. After World War I, the electrical and communications equipment industries secured a major start in the area. The electronic developments of World War II have improved some of these products and other technological improvements have increased the demand for other local products. Heavy engineering works and machine tool plants diversified their products as a result of war and postwar experience. The production of helicopters, initiated during the war, has continued. Chemical industries are undertaking the production of plastics, and, in a variety of other industries, new enterprises have started or facilities have been expanded.

The recent development of a basic steel works and expansion of metal-fabricating plants in the Greater Philadelphia Area are expected to give better balance to the local economic structure and yield higher purchasing power in the region. This is but one example of heavy capital outlays in the area since the close of World War II in a wide variety of industries. It is estimated that between 1945 and 1955, capital expenditures by industry for new plants and equipment totaled nearly six billion dollars in the eleven counties in Pennsylvania, New Jersey, and Delaware that comprise the Delaware Valley region. This rate of capital expenditure compares favorably with that of other expanding sections of the nation.[24]

The war brought substantial population gains to the city of Philadelphia and its environs, although some population was lost to the city immediately after the end of the war and the city's permanent gains were less substantial than those of its surrounding counties. According to the 1950 Census of Population, the gains from 1940 to 1950 were 7 per cent for the city, as compared with 15 per cent for the eight-county area.

Although wartime changes in the demand for labor created significant shifts in the industrial and occupational structure of employment in Philadelphia, they were of short duration, and, in the long-term setting of the decades reviewed in this report, did not alter the direction of underlying trends. Relative to population, local employment trends followed those in nonagricultural employment in the nation relative to nonfarm population except that the local decline in manufacturing was much greater than in the United States. Nor did war and postwar changes modify a persistent downward trend in the demand for production workers, service workers, and proprietors relative to population or the upward trend for clerical and professional workers, trends that had characterized Philadelphia in the decades from 1910 to 1940.

[24] *Greater Philadelphia Magazine* (Chamber of Commerce of Greater Philadelphia), June 1954, p. 24.

These findings have implications for the city's educational, vocational guidance, and placement programs, for policies initiated by employers and trade unions that may affect the competitive position of Philadelphia's industries or the operation of the labor market, as well as for general economic planning in the community. Moreover, they strengthen the view that nation-wide changes in the demand for goods and services, in the location of industry and population, and in the skill requirements of industry have far-reaching effects on the industrial life of metropolitan centers. Adaptations of a local labor force to such changes may have the appearance of being effectuated relatively easily, but they require more than the direction of young workers to expanding rather than contracting fields of employment. They require shifts by experienced workers to other lines of work or to other communities, earlier retirement from the labor market than may have been expected, or the entrance to the labor market of other members of a family when the chief wage earner can no longer secure a job. Major shifts of this nature are effectuated at relatively minor social costs when employment levels are high, but are difficult when the volume of unemployment rises substantially. The implications of Philadelphia's long-term experience for economic development planning in cities and for solving problems of effective labor utilization in a community are discussed in the concluding chapter.

Chapter VII

Economic Development Problems and Employment Policy in Cities

PRECEDING CHAPTERS have outlined the major trends of recent decades in Philadelphia with respect to levels of economic activity, rates of growth, and accompanying changes in the structure of the economy and of the labor force. Comparisons with national experience and that of other cities have suggested that some aspects of these developments were peculiar to Philadelphia by reason of its location or specialized economic activities. Other aspects appear to have been common to the nation as a whole or to its largest cities. The interpretation of these changes has been outlined in earlier chapters and the findings will be recapitulated in terms of the broader implications of Philadelphia's experience.

These broader implications may be stated as questions to which the evidence for Philadelphia may suggest answers. Is there evidence, for example, of a growth pattern for cities comparable to the growth pattern that has been suggested for industries? Supplementing this general question are considerations of the impact of changes in the location of population and industry on the growth of cities, the position of mature as compared with younger cities in the national economy, and the significance for future economic prospects of a slowing-down of growth in the area or region of which a city is the largest center. Does the concentration of specific types of business activity in a metropolitan center make it highly vulnerable to business-cycle changes? Conversely, does diversification of activity spread such risks? Are recent changes in the economic functions of cities likely to increase or decrease their vulnerability? What are the implications of Philadelphia's experience for planning the economic development of cities?

Changes in the labor force that accompany change in the levels and distribution of employment also raise questions of broader economic or social significance than considerations for any particular city. Such questions concern the degree of flexibility of the labor force in making adaptations to cyclical and structural changes in the economy and the relation of employment policy to planning economic development. Is there evidence, for example, that the labor force contracts in a depression and expands in prosperity? Does its structure change with changes in size? Through what labor-force channels is employment redistributed among occupations or industries? Can public and private training and placement policy retard or accelerate such changes? Is the solution of structural unemployment problems primarily a national or local and regional responsibility?

Growth Patterns of Cities

It is now well established that the development of trade and transportation had important effects on the origin and early growth of cities and that the development of manufacturing paced their development at later stages. But urbanization of the population continued after the industrialization of the economy, resulting in continued growth of the largest cities of the nation as well as in the rise of new centers. Philadelphia's experience in this regard is typical of many cities.

Writing in the early thirties, McLaughlin summarized what he considered to be the major factors in the growth of the nation's largest industrial areas. He found that, in general, the areas in which manufacturing had expanded most rapidly up to that time were those dominated by new industries or very rapid population growth, as in Detroit and Los Angeles. Widely diversified activities were accompanied by slower rates of growth, as in Philadelphia. Areas specializing in capital goods increased more rapidly prior to 1900, while consumers' goods centers increased more rapidly after that date. The size of the economic hinterland or marketing area served by a given city also affected its rate of growth. In addition, there were regional or local differences in leadership and the character of business organization or the degree of absentee ownership of local enterprise that directly or indirectly affected the competitive position of a community in specific industries.[1]

Possible causes of a slow rate of growth in Philadelphia as compared with other cities therefore might be the diversifiication of its economic activities, its sharing with other cities the servicing of a region that is, in part, common to all of them, and possibly, the conservative character of its business and financial practices that stressed limited investment risks. To this list of influences, one might add changes in the relative importance of the region in which the city is located. Despite the fact that within the same economic region cities have experienced widely differing rates of growth, it is possible that the cumulative effect of population and economic changes in a region may from time to time overshadow the influences peculiar to its leading city.

The New England and Middle Atlantic states just prior to World War II, for example, had 27 per cent of the total population and 40 per cent of the manufacturing wage earners of the nation. By contrast, in 1900, they had had approximately the same proportion of the nation's population but over half of the factory wage earners.[2] Their relative share of industrial activity had declined during this period, although they have continued to grow with the nation. Eastern capital and people built up the West and a natural sequence of this development was a decline in the relative importance of Eastern Seaboard communities in the nation, with the exception of New York City, which has continued to maintain its position as the nation's leading metropolis. This change in relative position is exemplified by the rapid rise of Chicago to displace Philadelphia as second among the largest cities and by more recent challenges by Detroit and Los Angeles to Philadelphia's position as the third largest center. These changes in its relative position in the nation are of long standing and, as a commentator on New England's position in the national economy remarked, one "to which it has become accustomed after a couple of hundred years."[3]

It is, perhaps, too soon to understand fully what a region's relative

---

1 Glen McLaughlin, *Growth of American Manufacturing Areas* (Pittsburgh: University of Pittsburgh Press, 1938), pp. 199-237.

2 U. S. Departments of Commerce and Agriculture, *Changes in Distribution of Manufacturing Wage Earners, 1899-1939* (Washington, 1942), pp. 24-30.

3 *The Philadelphia Inquirer,* January 3, 1949.

loss of position in the national economy means for the long-term economic prospects of its metropolitan centers. There is evidence in Philadelphia's experience that the continued effects of a slowing-down in population and economic growth in a region may set up a chain reaction on income levels and job opportunities in the industries primarily dependent on local population that indirectly affect a city's competitive position. On favorable assumptions of the ability of the city and its region to maintain their historic share of the nation's population, it was estimated not long ago that the Philadelphia-Camden area would reach its maximum population in 1980.[4] Although it was recognized that unforeseen events might easily push this date nearer or further away, Philadelphia is not the only city likely to reach this stage in the span of another generation.

Changes in the Functions of Cities

The drift of populations to urban centers is a phenomenon of all industrialized countries and this country has been no exception. Between 1900 and 1950, the nation's population doubled while the urban population gained by tenfold. In 1900, there were only 6 cities of 500,000 population or over but by 1950, there were 18. The metropolitan districts of these large cities accounted for 32 per cent of the total population of the country and 42 per cent of the nation's employment in manufacturing in 1950.

Servicing the wants of large populations has modified the economic structure of metropolitan communities. Dependence on manufacturing as a source of income has declined, relatively if not absolutely, and a myriad of service activities have increased in relative importance. Colin Clark describes this change as follows:

> Cities remain and find new functions when the purpose for which they were established has become partially or completely obsolete. It is a commonplace that cities first established for purposes of defense or as communication centers developed

[4] Philadelphia City Planning Commission, *Population Estimates, Philadelphia-Camden Area, 1950-2000,* Planning Study No. 1, April 1948, p. 3. On the other hand, a prominent realtor in the city estimated in 1951 that the population of the Philadelphia-Camden-Trenton area is likely to increase to 4 to 6 million in the next two decades, as a result of proposed expansion of steel and metal-fabricating industries and oil refining, and greater use of port facilities.—Philadelphia, *Chamber of Commerce News,* March 19, 1951, p. 3.

> into centers of manufacture when their original function became of minor importance. It is not so generally realized, however, that the manufacturing city is now, in its turn, giving place to one whose principal function is the carrying-on of service industries.[5]

Although the economic base of cities has been modified by the development of service activities, there is no indication that they are less vulnerable to economic catastrophe by reason of that fact. "The tenuousness of the urban economy, which expresses itself particularly in the rapid and cumulative effects of depressions, is actually a characteristic that is basic to urban life generally."[6] A major proportion of the labor force of cities is dependent on wage or salary jobs, and the spiraling effects of a depression appear to be accentuated in large population centers. During the thirties, for example, 20 per cent of the total population on relief rolls was concentrated in the 10 largest cities,[7] which had 15 per cent of the nation's population in 1940.

Despite the changes that occur as cities undertake new functions or adapt to changes in the national economy, there is a notable stability in the basic structure of a city's economy. A textile center may add new types of service or production activity, but it seldom becomes a steel-producing center. A diversified manufacturing center infrequently becomes a specialized center. An East Coast city does not take on the industrial characteristics of a West Coast city. This stability of basic structure in local economies arises from the pattern of national development of commerce and industry in which advantage was taken of an area's resources and location and a permanent imprint made on the economic life of cities and, hence, of the nation. Philadelphia's experience in this regard is noteworthy. Despite substantial declines in employment in textile manufacturing, for example, in 1950 it had a higher proportion of total employment in textiles than any city of 250,000 population or over, except Atlanta, Georgia. Its natural advantages for shipbuilding are utilized whenever there is a rising demand for shipping. It has retained char-

5 Colin Clark, "The Economic Functions of a City in Relation to its Size," *Econometrica*, April 1945, p. 97.

6 National Resources Committee, *Our Cities: Their Role in the National Economy* (Washington, June 1937), p. 55.

7 *Ibid.*, p. 14.

acteristics of its early start in manufacturing metal products despite shifts in the relative importance of various types of products. Although there has been expansion in various types of nonmanufacturing activity, the local economy still rests primarily on a manufacturing base.

While a city takes on new functions as it broadens services for a larger local population, its basic functions in the national economy are determined by its "export" industries, that is to say, by those segments of manufacturing, transportation, and trade or other services that produce for regional and national or international markets. It is in these industries that expansion or contraction and competitive advantages or disadvantages have importance for gauging future prospects.

Vulnerability of Cities to Structural and Cyclical Changes

The downward swing in manufacturing employment in Philadelphia and its environs between World Wars I and II reversed the trend of the decades up to 1920, and was itself reversed during the forties. In most instances, local factory employment followed national trends, but the community was vulnerable on two scores. The production demands of World War I had led to overexpansion of heavy munitions industries, particularly shipbuilding, followed by extensive layoffs in the postwar years. The naval disarmament program and the decline in the American Merchant Marine aggravated this situation locally. Much the same experience was repeated during and after World War II. Employment in the area tends to gain rapidly during a war but shrinks rapidly when peace comes. In nondurable goods industries, Philadelphia had and continues to have a relatively high proportion of total manufacturing employment in the textile and apparel industries as compared with other cities. In the years under review, a number of changes occurred that adversely affected the competitive position of local textile industries and resulted in a net loss of nearly half of the textile jobs available in 1910. This loss was offset by employment gains in other industries but was never regained in textile manufacturing. The area has therefore been vulnerable to changes in the location of the textile industries and to changes in technology and consumption habits that have affected the demand for labor in the specialized branches of the textile industries represented in the area.

The most striking structural changes that occurred in the Philadelphia area in the years under review were shifts from the production of durable to nondurable goods in manufacturing after World Wars I and II and an increase in the relative importance of nonmanufacturing industries as a source of employment between 1910 and 1950. Presumably, these structural changes might make the area less vulnerable to extreme fluctuations in employment resulting from business-cycle changes. The trends in local employment followed national trends, but Philadelphia gained less than the nation in rapidly expanding industries and lost more heavily than the nation in the older manufacturing industries in which employment was contracting. A growing differential between national and local rates of growth or decline in manufacturing was paralleled in some service activities. In this connection, it may be noted again that for some types of nonmanufacturing activity, Philadelphia shares with New York, and to a limited extent with Baltimore, the servicing of a region of relatively small geographic compass, although it is a densely populated, highly industrialized, and relatively wealthy region.

Planning for the Economic Development of Cities

Cities and their environs continue to offer locational advantages to business enterprise because they offer some of the economies of large-scale operations, such as a flexible and relatively skilled labor force and a variety of business services, as well as ready access to consumers. Moreover, large and well-established industrial centers continue to "play a leading part as the germinating grounds for new industries,"[8] as they have in the past. Recent technological developments have increasingly freed industries from earlier restrictions with respect to location and there are substantial numbers of "footloose" industries for which all population centers are competitors. It is possible that locational shifts of industry and consequent changes in the economic structure of metropolitan centers may be more frequent in the future than they have been in the past. A community must therefore look to its own past as well as to future prospects in

8 E. M. Hoover, *The Location of Economic Activity* (New York: McGraw-Hill Book Co., 1948), p. 176.

the nation to gauge its relative economic advantages or disadvantages in competition with other cities.

The economic development programs of cities are likely to place too much emphasis on the attraction of *new* industries and *additional* population per se. It appears equally important for a city to make sure that its present industries are adequately served and that all precautions to retain and promote the welfare of those industries are met, insofar as community leadership and action can serve these ends. If stability of business organization and economic structure is of value to a community, and there is every reason to believe that this is the case, every effort should be made to provide the community with adequate knowledge about its economic structure and competitive position as a basis for promoting such stability.

There is a tendency also for economic development programs in cities to stress the value of diversification, per se. There is no doubt but that while the "advantages of specialization go largely to the specializers,"[9] the diversification of economic activity may spread the risks of adversity in a community. Nevertheless, from the national point of view one may well ask whether the national economy, and indirectly local economies, will be better off if every region or area becomes highly diversified. In the development of the nation's manufactures and trade, specialization and localization of economic activity have offered definite economic advantages and the relative stability of differences in the economic structure of cities over time testifies to the enduring quality of these advantages. Our largest cities certainly respond to long-term trends in national growth and prosperity, and their very size may make them extremely sensitive to cyclical and secular changes.[10] Philadelphia, for all of its diversification of economic activity, has not been immune to extremely severe unemployment during depressions, nor to major changes in its structure.

Pittsburgh, with the highest rate and longest duration of unemployment of any of our largest cities in 1940, offers a good case in point. The aftermath of the depression of the thirties was to leave its community leaders with a strong feeling that economic activity in the area must become diversified, and local development programs

---

9 *Ibid.*, p. 285.
10 National Resources Committee, *Our Cities.*

emphasized this objective.[11] Following the basing-point decision on steel prices, however, several metal-fabricating plants moved into the Pittsburgh area to take advantage of cheaper steel, and recent diversification has, in fact, taken the form of expansion of the established metal industries.[12] Even though this development was in a sense "accidental," it challenges the relative merits of policies encouraging diversification for its own sake as against the expansion or supplementation of an established structure.

This is just another way of saying that in planning for economic development there are few, if any, general formulas that can be successfully applied to all communities. Cyclically unstable industries exist and "must find a home somewhere."[13] While it would be advantageous for all communities to have some representation of new and rapidly expanding industries, the number of such industries is limited and their location determined by many factors. The Philadelphia area, for example, has had a relatively high concentration of the nation's recent production of television and electronic equipment, but this development is attributable to the pioneering work of the established radio industry and its relatively large-scale facilities. Few communities could offer comparable facilities for this developmental work.

Industries with a high proportion of payroll to total costs are advantageous to a community because they exert a relatively large "leverage" effect on consumer incomes. All communities would like to have such industries, but not all industries have high ratios of payrolls to total production costs. Under certain circumstances, the expansion of low labor-cost industries may bring advantages to a community. The Delaware River Basin, for example, is the largest oil refining center in the nation if not in the world. [14] Oil refining is a low labor-cost industry, but in addition to affording more employment in oil refining and stimulating research and development in related chemical industries that are notably important in the area, this expansion will yield a more intensive use of available port facili-

11 *Business Week*, July 5, 1947, p. 57; *New York Times*, May 2, 1946, December 19, 1947.

12 *The Evening Bulletin* (Philadelphia), January 15, 1949.

13 Hoover, *op. cit.*, p. 287.

14 "This is Greater Philadelphia," *The Evening Bulletin* (Philadelphia), January 13, 1954.

ties and strengthen the prewar specialization of port traffic. Extreme specialization of port traffic may have some local disadvantages, but, from the national point of view, it may further the most effective utilization of East Coast ports and eventually yield more local advantages than disadvantages.

A recent report of the Philadelphia City Planning Commission makes a recommendation that is designed to promote selective expansion of manufacturing activity in this area.[15] Certain industries were cited as especially advantageous because of their prospective rates of growth, relative cyclical and seasonal stability, use of skilled workers, average wages and salaries paid, and appropriateness to the future economy. The industries so selected are: electrical machinery and light electrical equipment, iron and steel fabrication, light metal fabrication, professional and scientific instruments, chemicals, plastics, publishing and printing, quick frozen foods, liquors and beverages, and biscuits and bakery products. Several of these industries are already well established in the Philadelphia area; all meet the criteria suggested by the Planning Commission; most cities would presumably gain from increased production of these items in their respective areas.

Expansion in the selected industries might bring relatively greater economic advantages to the Philadelphia area than a comparable expansion in other types of factory employment. Nevertheless, the community should not overlook the need for encouraging expansion or preventing declines in employment in manufacturing industries that do not necessarily meet the suggested criteria but are ones in which the city's locational quotient was high in 1950. For various reasons or combinations of reasons, some 24 manufacturing industries have found locational advantages that have persisted over decades. In turn, they constitute the source of the city's chief factory "exports" and provide the wherewithal for the community to trade with the rest of the world. This group of industries includes some which are not mentioned for official encouragement, namely, several types of textile products and apparel, paper products, shipbuilding, railroad, and miscellaneous transportation equipment, tanning and leather products (except footwear), a variety of food and chemical

---

15 Philadelphia City Planning Commission, *Economic Base Study of the Philadelphia Area,* August 1949, pp. 38-39.

products, and oil refining. The fortunes of these industries are inextricably interwoven with the prospective competitive position of the area in the national economy and, as such, merit some attention in a development program.

These comments should not be interpreted as meaning that city or regional planning is not necessary or desirable. One of the inevitable consequences of the nation's economic progress is the rise of new industries and the decline of old, or the relocation of economic activities and consequent shifts in the absolute or relative position of various centers of production. Mitigating the social costs of such changes is a justifiable and desirable objective of public policy. Moreover, the area in which conscious locational policy can operate is widening and full advantage of such opportunities should be taken. What is needed is greater unanimity of opinion with respect to the objectives of city, regional, and national planning in relation to the operation of a free market economy and more knowledge of historical factors in the geographic impact of national cyclical and structural changes.

On the basis of improved knowledge, it should be possible to find a parent corporation for a promising local business enterprise that needs an infusion of new blood and capital, or marketing research facilities for a group of small firms that make a highly specialized and intermediate type of product for a limited market. Such knowledge may also widen the horizons of business leaders, when the stake in the development of new enterprises or the salvaging of old is greater than the immediate financial risks involved. The maintenance of high levels of productivity becomes a bulwark of the competitive position of mature plants in an industry, and labor unions as well as business enterprises have responsibilities for the maintenance of the competitive position of established local industries. In the negotiation of many collective bargaining agreements, Philadelphia plants or industries are considered "marginal," either because they are small and highly specialized or because local agreements tend to follow, with minor exceptions, the patterns established elsewhere. The decisions that are basic to these agreements, however, are not "marginal" to Philadelphia employers and workers and they should be continuously reviewed for their effect on production costs and employment in the area.

As in the case of all large cities, the solution of problems of traffic congestion, of land-use in the central sections of the city, and of zoning or rezoning for industrial use is a factor in effective planning for economic growth. Moreover, improvement and expansion of port and other facilities for the Delaware River Valley require the cooperation of local governments in three states, without any effective governmental machinery for such cooperation. Business leadership has sponsored a number of joint ventures in developmental activities on a broad geographic base but these ventures will eventually need more support from both private and public sources.

That further economic changes will take place is inevitable. Technological developments continue to flow from research and engineering laboratories. New products displace old and new processes render obsolete present equipment and skills. Population shifts create new centers of consumption and economic activity and modify the relative importance of older centers. Moreover, as the nation exhausts its supply of natural resources, it turns to foreign sources of supply, as in the case of iron ore and oil. The relative importance of seaboard as compared with inland communities will be affected by this type of shift. Changes in international relations policy and the industrialization of undeveloped countries will affect the export markets for American products and the volume and character of imports. In turn, some producing centers may experience expanding employment while it declines in others. Shifts in the distribution of national, regional, and local employment are, therefore, to be expected and the anticipation of and planning for such changes constitute an important aspect of economic development programs in general.

Demographic and Economic Factors in Labor-Force Dynamics

Just as enterprises in the city of Philadelphia and its environs have had to meet an altered demand for goods and services in the region and nation, so has the local labor force adjusted to an ever-changing economic environment. Its inherent resiliency is attested to in the preceding chapters. Although it is widely recognized that both demographic and socio-economic factors have played a significant role in labor-force dynamics, there is some disagreement as to the relative importance of these influences.

Wolfbein and Jaffe found that the major factors in national labor-force growth between 1890 and 1930 were socio-economic rather than demographic in character,[16] and Durand's more intensive analysis for the period from 1920 to 1940 substantiates this finding.[17] The socio-economic factors noted by Durand and other writers as important influences are changes in the structure of the demand for labor, increased income and rising standards of living and leisure, and changes in social custom, particularly with respect to the retirement of older workers, longer schooling for young workers, and the growing acceptance of women in gainful employment. Some demographic influences, if not offset by nondemographic, would have had the effect of reducing the size of the national labor force during these decades. On the other hand, Long found that when the experience of this and other countries over six decades is standardized for comparative purposes, the over-all rates of labor-force participation are remarkably stable, and that such changes as occur show little, if any, association with changes in income and employment levels.[18]

When one turns to the experience of cities, economic influences appear to play a predominant role, partly because the economies of cities differ substantially from that of the nation at any given time and change more rapidly over time. Moreover, their rates of population growth appear to be more markedly influenced by economic circumstances, whether of national or local origin. Labor-force participation rates in cities are usually higher than those of the country as a whole but vary from city to city. Schoenberg and Douglas[19] and Long[20] found negative association between average income and the proportion of the population in the labor force of cities in 1929 and in 1940, respectively. Belloc found that the labor-force participation of women in 91 cities was associated with the income levels of male workers and the industrial structure of cities.[21]

---

16 Seymour L. Wolfbein and Abram J. Jaffe, "Demographic Factors in Labor Force Growth," *American Sociological Review*, August 1946, p. 394.

17 John D. Durand, *The Labor Force in the United States, 1890-1960* (New York: Social Science Research Council, 1948), chaps. 3 and 4.

18 Clarence D. Long, *Labor Force, Income, and Employment* (mimeographed manuscript for the National Bureau of Economic Research, 1950).

19 Erika H. Schoenberg and Paul H. Douglas, "Studies in the Supply Curve of Labor: The Relation in 1929 between Average Earnings in American Cities and the Proportions Seeking Employment," *Journal of Political Economy*, December 1937, pp. 45-79.

20 Long, *op. cit.*, pp. 14-22.

General acceptance of a negative association between income and labor-force propensities in cities at a given point of time is noted because it has led some persons to assume that the same kind of relationship might hold over time. If valid, one would expect the labor force to increase in a depression when income falls and decrease in a prosperous period when income rises. Such a theory was posited, at least for depression conditions, on the character of some of the changes that occurred among various groups in the labor force during the thirties.[22] The statistical evidence, however, does not support the view that *total* unemployment during a depression is swollen by persons whose entrance to the labor market is forced by the unemployment of usual breadwinners. On the contrary, the available evidence suggests that the net effects of a depression combine to reduce the size of the labor force through increased rates of retirement by older workers and postponement of entrance to the labor market by young persons. Moreover, in cities, substantial population losses may occur during a depression through an overbalance of out-migration over natural increase and in-migration; these losses further reduce the size of a city's labor-force.

Despite relatively small changes in the rates of labor-force participation by the total population 14 years of age and over, substantial changes have occurred in the age, sex, and marital status of workers and the ways in which families have participated in the labor force. Despite higher rates of retirement, the labor force has grown older as a result of increased longevity and other changes in the age composition of the population. In addition, relatively large numbers of women have entered the labor force in recent decades while young persons have continued schooling for longer periods. These changes, in turn, have affected the pattern of family participation in the labor force in the largest cities.

Philadelphia's experience in these respects followed national urban trends. The only special circumstances to be noted are that the city has for many decades had a relatively large number of women in its labor force and a relatively high proportion of families with more

---

21 Nedra B. Belloc, "Labor-Force Participation and Employment Opportunities for Women," *Journal of the American Statistical Association*, September 1950, pp. 400-10.

22 W. S. Woytinsky, *Three Aspects of Labor Dynamics* (Washington: Social Science Research Council, 1942), chap. XV.

than one worker. These attributes appear to be associated with the sex, age, and racial composition of its population and the character of economic activities in the community. Relatively high labor-force rates at all times imply that to meet high production demands during a war, Philadelphia is dependent on the attraction of workers from outside the area to supplement its labor force. During World War II, for example, more workers were added to the city's labor force through in-migration than through increased rates of labor-force participation. If recent cyclical experience is indicative, Philadelphia and other large cities tend to lose more population than they gain through migration in a depression and the reverse occurs in a prosperous period. On the other hand, persistently high labor-force rates, together with wide diversification of manufacturing or other economic activities, provide the city with a labor supply that is experienced in a variety of activities and relatively adaptable to changes in the distribution of employment.

Changes in the Distribution of Employment and Labor Mobility

Fluctuations in the levels of employment in different industries and occupations occur within a year and from year to year, as well as from decade to decade. The net changes that account for a redistribution of employment over several decades therefore understate substantially the total number and kinds of job shifts that are made by a community's labor force. Nevertheless, the trends reflected in such net gains or losses provide a measure of basic changes in the structure of employment that affect the character of future labor requirements and indicate the role played by the mobility of labor.

National changes from 1910 to 1950 highlighted a major shift of employment relative to population from the primary or extractive industries to manufacturing and services. During the same period, there were also substantial changes in the demand for workers with given grades of skill that modified the distribution of employment by occupational groups, independently of what might have been expected from a change in the distribution of employment by industry alone. Both types of changes reduced the demand for "manual" as compared with white-collar workers and afforded expanding opportunity for the employment of women. More precisely, the demand for clerical and professional and related workers and operatives increased persistently in the nation relative to nonfarm population, while the demand for workers in other occupational groups declined.

Local developments in labor requirements between 1910 and 1950 in most instances paralleled national developments. Employment in the occupational groups in which older workers predominate, namely the skilled crafts and proprietary groups, did not keep pace with population growth. Moreover, the occupations in which Negroes usually enter the labor market, namely unskilled labor and domestic service, declined heavily relative to population growth. Local trends in the employment of women also paralleled those in the nation, although the gains in total employment of women were less substantial. Both because Philadelphia industries have employed women since the early days of the factory system, and because factory employment, particularly that of operatives, did not keep pace with population growth, the local increase in the numbers of women employed between 1910 and 1950 was less than one-third as great as the national increase.

These findings suggest that opportunities in professional, semiprofessional, and clerical occupations will continue to provide job opportunities for an increasing proportion of the city's labor force. Variations in general employment levels and the rate of future expansion of manufacturing will affect the degree of opportunity for craftsmen, operatives, and the proprietary group to a greater extent than for other occupational groups. Local employment for service workers and laborers, on the other hand, is likely to offer steadily declining opportunity. Future technological changes are likely to increase the numbers of technicians and specialists required in industries where "automation" may develop. It is, however, too early to judge the extent to which such changes will modify the occupational structure of Philadelphia in the near future.

Long-term changes in the structure of employment are effectuated through the medium of recruitment of young people to expanding industries or occupations and the retirement or transfer of workers attached to declining industries and occupations. A variety of influences will accelerate or retard this process. The transitions are easier if general employment levels are high and more difficult if there is a large volume of unemployment. The transferability of specific skills, training, or experience from industry to industry will influence the ease with which individuals can make the necessary shifts. If the average age of workers in declining occupations and industries is high, a policy of no replacements for retirements will gradually shrink the work force. If extensive layoffs occur, the older workers affected will have difficulty in securing other jobs, either because employers' hiring policies tend to discriminate against them in a market or because older workers are generally less mobile occupationally than younger workers.

The mobility of labor, in its broadest sense, is therefore the channel through which adaptations to changes in the structure of the economy take place. The labor market is never static; at any given time, some workers are in the process of changing jobs, of moving into or out of employment, or into or out of the labor force. The rate of labor turnover varies between men and women, old and young, and skilled and unskilled, but operates to create job opportunities over and above net requirements. There is evidence that retirements from the labor force are a more important source of job openings than a net increase in employment and that movement between jobs may create more job openings than labor-force turnover.[23] Replacement ratios that take account of both net and gross requirements are known to vary between industries and occupations, but present knowledge about these differences is extremely limited. A strong upward trend in the demand for clerical workers, combined with a relatively high labor turnover among young women who constitute the majority of such workers, has accounted for a constant increase in gross as well as net employment in the clerical occupations. As a result, the widespread shift from training for factory to clerical occupations for girls has had a sound economic base in fact. Other occupations, however, have had a different trend in demand or employ workers in other age and sex groups and therefore present a different outlook for future gross employment. More knowledge of the potential mobility and work-life expectancy fac-

23 Daniel Carson, "Occupational Mobility and Occupational Outlook," *The Southern Economic Journal*, April 1948, pp. 411-19.

tors in various occupations as well as of long-term trends in demand is needed, before adequate plans for training, counselling, and placing workers can be developed in a community. Such knowledge is important also for assessing the availability of labor in relation to requirements at different levels of economic activity in a plant, an industry, or a community.

It should be noted that social institutions exercise an important role in accelerating or retarding the mobility of the labor force. The availability and quality of training, counselling, and placement programs in a community, the hiring policies of employers, the entrance restrictions, seniority rules, and other policies of trade unions, and public legislation all play a part in facilitating the adaptations of workers to an ever-changing economic environment. Many institutional practices appear to reflect customary attitudes in a community. Relatively little is known, for example, about the efficiency of or incidence of accidents among older as compared with young workers in different types of industries, although the hiring practices of employers tend to discriminate against older workers on grounds of inefficiency and accident hazard.[24] Again, the apprenticeship ratios in many unionized crafts reflect the practice of previous years and are not changed to meet new conditions in the average age of workers in the craft or in the demand for the specific type of labor concerned. Because freedom of occupational choice is an important "right" in a democratic society, vocational aspirations do not necessarily reflect the aptitudes of individuals in terms of hiring specifications of the job market. In response to the demand of students or their parents, vocational schools may continue programs of training for jobs that offer relatively declining opportunities or for which the training requirements may be obsolescent. Social custom and community attitudes also play an important part in discriminatory practices that affect the employment of minority religious or nationality and racial groups in a population.[25] The provisions of

---

24 See Max D. Kossoris, "Absenteeism and Injury Experience of Old Workers," *Monthly Labor Review*, July 1948, pp. 16-19, for evidence to the effect that the frequency rates of injuries are highest below age 45. See also A. T. Welford and D. Speakman, "Employability of Older People," Part III of *The Aged and Society, edited by Milton Derber* (Industrial Relations Research Association, 1950), pp. 181-203.

25 E. William Noland and E. Wight Bakke, *Workers Wanted: A Study of*

relief or unemployment compensation legislation and subsequent administrative practices may discourage the movement of workers across state boundaries or between industries. Although little is known about the concrete effect of such institutional practices, many of them would appear to retard the mobility of labor, either directly or indirectly.

The community has an interest in the effective utilization of its labor supply, since ineffective use gives rise to social costs that may take the form of increased public assistance or unemployment compensation loads, and possible population loss. Moreover, productive efficiency is one of the keys to the maintenance of a city's competitive position in the national economy as well as to income and employment levels in the community. An important factor in productive efficiency is the size and adaptability of the labor force and the quality of its contribution to the community's productive effort. That contribution is high when persons who are able and willing to work have jobs and the jobs afford maximum use of their experience and skills. This result is more readily achieved if the mobility of labor is accelerated rather than retarded by the social institutions that operate in the labor market.

Patterns of Labor-Market Behavior

Research of the past two decades has refined statistical measures for describing what happens in the labor market and for delineating changes in trends or differences between groups of workers in broad outlines. Despite evidence of the existence of behavior patterns, we know little about why such changes or differences occur or why individuals or groups behave as they do. The explanation of these behavior patterns is central to the task of future research in this field. We know, for example, that there are differences between cities in the employment of women, or of married women, and that these differences are associated statistically with certain demographic or economic phenomena, but we do not know what motivations account for the differences in pattern, or whether the "pushes" of adversity are more important than the "pulls" of opportunity. Again,

Employers' Hiring Policies, Preferences, and Practices in New Haven and Charlotte (New York: Harper & Brothers, 1949).

we know that workers voluntarily change jobs for a variety of reasons or combinations of reasons. But whether these changes reflect the conscious pursuit of an occupational career or whether such planning is a luxury not indulged in by the average worker is not known.

These unanswered questions have more than academic import: they are central to finding the right answer to a number of important problems of public policy. If a nation becomes involved in a war when employment levels are high and most persons who are readily available for work have jobs, the successful recruitment of additional workers hinges upon a knowledge of motivations with respect to the labor market. If major shifts of manpower from less essential to war industries have to be planned and executed, they will not be successful if there is little or no knowledge of the circumstances under which workers change jobs in peacetime or of the kinds of workers for whom job shifts can be most readily planned. Even if legislation provides rigid and total manpower controls, the planning and execution of an effective mobilization program in a democratic society requires more knowledge of labor-market behavior than we have to date.

Nor is the usefulness of better knowledge about behavior patterns in the labor market limited to emergency situations, as during a war. Success in many aspects of the personnel programs of employers, the employment policies of trade unions, and the training and placement of workers by public agencies devolves upon better knowledge of factors in job and occupational attachments. These programs are based on erroneous premises, if the majority of workers gain no sense of vocational attachment or accomplishment after spending years with a given employer, occupation, or industry. If workers believe that "all jobs are alike" and that advancement is largely a matter of accident, they will not take time to "learn a trade," endeavor to secure wider or better experience to improve their skills, or have much incentive to stay on a job or develop an occupational attachment. The attitudes of workers with respect to the labor market and to jobs have implications not only for the quality of future and current productivity but for other aspects of community welfare. One element of economic security in a community is the knowledge that a worker has a marketable skill at which he can earn a livelihood and that past or current investment in improving that skill will yield future dividends.

The experience of selected groups of factory workers in Philadelphia suggests that those who entered the labor market prior to the thirties had a considerable knowledge of the local job market and of relative differences in earnings between employers and industries. Their first jobs usually bore little relation to later work records and, during a depression, they might be forced to take any job that was available. For an older worker also, the most recent job held might bear little relation to his previous work history. On the whole, however, voluntary job changes over a ten-year period or a lifetime generally reflected a search for higher earnings, improved working conditions, wider experience, or other types of advancement, as workers viewed it. The opinions expressed did not necessarily connote either a preference for the specific type of work in which a man found himself or his initial vocational aspirations, but, over time, the majority had gained a sense of attachment to or identification with an occupation or type of work. For workers with highly specialized skills, which may not have been readily transferable, this sense of attachment may have been a matter of necessity, but strong attachments were also found for multiple-type or less specialized skills. Many Philadelphia factory workers who entered the labor market prior to the thirties believed in the desirability of learning a "trade," in the sense of a craft or a skilled machine operation, or had followed the advice of their parents in this regard. Moreover, long service with one employer was occasionally noted as a desirable kind of experience.

Workers who entered the labor market during the thirties and forties have had unusual interruptions to their experience and may have developed different attitudes to jobs and work careers. During the depression, the rate of unemployment was especially high for young people, both because they were in relatively large supply as compared with earlier decades (as a result of high birth rates during World War I), and because experienced workers could be readily secured from among the ranks of the unemployed. Few, if any, apprentices were trained during this period and the available jobs offered less opportunity for advancement. Although many young workers during the depression stayed in school longer, their attitudes toward the desirability of learning a "trade" were affected by widespread unemployment in all grades of occupations. After 1940, World War II and the Korean crisis interrupted the vocational careers of young men. Moreover, the opportunity to secure civilian jobs at relatively high earnings with little or no experience may have had some effect on the labor-market attitudes of young workers who were not old enough to serve in the armed forces. In any event, difficulties have been reported in recruiting learners and apprentices for some types of work in the postwar years, and employers and vocational counsellors complain of high turnover and "restlessness" among young workers.

Whether there has been a permanent change in the labor-market attitudes of today's workers as compared with earlier generations is not known, but it is well worth finding out. An appraisal of current attitudes is important not only for practical applications by employers, schools, or employment offices but also for implications with respect to wage theory and the allocation of manpower resources.[26]

Economic Development Planning and Employment Policy

Economic development or planning activities in cities may have several types of objectives but, in one way or another, they are concerned with maintaining or expanding employment levels. While a city is not in a position to exert a direct influence on fiscal or other general economic policies that affect the nation's level of employment, it should be in a position to know what the impact of national policies will be on its own economy. Moreover, it should be prepared to take maximum advantage of activities, such as public works or increased production for national defense, that will aid its economy. By the same token, a city should consider undertaking activities that will minimize the costs of implementation of national or international programs, such as changes in policies regarding the award of defense contracts or in tariff legislation, that may adversely affect its economy.

Not all changes that will affect the economy of a city, however,

---

26 See Herbert S. Parnes, *Research on Labor Mobility: An Appraisal of Research Findings in the United States* (New York: Social Science Research Council, 1954), chap. 5, for a discussion of conflicting findings of recent studies with respect to labor-market behavior.

are announced in public legislation. Less obvious changes in the distribution of population, in the location of industry, in the character and distribution of investment, or in the character and volume of the demand for goods and services in the nation will operate to alter the competitive position of a metropolitan area and its ability to attract and hold population. A community must take cognizance of these forces also and be prepared to exploit advantageous effects and to offset disadvantageous effects, or accept a modified role in the national economy. Variations in the levels of employment and in its distribution in metropolitan centers will flow from changes in the structure of the economy as well as from variations in the levels of business activity.

Long before the nation became concerned about the need for public acceptance of some responsibilty for employment policy, cities were aware of the need for continuous information on employment and unemployment and for activities that would alleviate the economic distress of their residents. Employment policy has therefore been a matter of concern to cities for many decades. Although their authority is limited because many generating influences are external to their sphere of jurisdiction, cities still have a significant role to play. It takes the form of facilitating expansion or mitigating the effects of contraction and thus of maximizing the utilization of the resident labor force. Qualitative as well as quantitative aspects of labor utilization are involved and schools and colleges, placement and counselling services, employers and labor unions in their daily activities determine the employment policy of a city.

For Philadelphia, as for other cities, there are three groups in the labor supply with the conditions of whose employment community-wide public policy should be particularly concerned. The training, counselling, and placement of young people will continue to play an important role in determining the quality of the future labor force, as they have in the past. Community resources are usually more adequate for this task than for others, but program objectives need to be integrated into general community planning with respect to employment policy. Moreover, until the babies born during the forties grow up, young workers will be in relatively short supply and therefore in a more-favored position in the job market. The other two groups needing particular attention are older workers and Negroes. In both cases, there are aspects of supply and demand that create special problems. Older persons and Negroes are becoming a relatively larger group in the population and in the labor force of the Philadelphia area while job opportunities for them are shrinking, both because of persistent declines in the occupations that usually employ them and because hiring practices tend to discriminate against their employment in specific situations. Legislation respecting "fair" employment practices may alleviate the most obvious aspects of discriminatory hiring practices with respect to minority population groups, but there are many ways by which the intent of such legislation can be circumvented. More constructive policies are needed both for minority population groups and for older workers. The widened range of job opportunities for Negroes that is found in the unionized needle trades should be followed in other industries, and wartime experience with the successful employment of older workers has significance for peacetime pursuits. The facts about long-term changes in the structure of the labor force and in the demand for labor should be faced realistically by the community and provided for in civic endeavors.

It may be noted that whenever labor is relatively scarce, as during a war, hiring specifications are relaxed in order to secure workers. Then the problems of employment for older workers or minority population groups tend to be more readily resolved. "Full" employment of the labor force may not guarantee that all workers are employed at their maximum skills, but it does tend to assure that all persons available for work have jobs. It is in periods of a slowing down of economic activity or in a depression that hiring specifications become more rigid and that some groups in the labor force receive preferential treatment.

In addition to those groups in the labor force among whom the incidence of unemployment may be relatively high at all times, there are occasions when structural unemployment becomes the outstanding problem in a community. One has only to cite the longstanding problems of the anthracite mining counties of Pennsylvania and recent unemployment among New England and Philadelphia textile workers to illustrate this problem. These situations may or may not be important enough to influence the national figures on unemployment but they are highly significant to local communities.

The kinds of economic policies envisaged in the Employment Act of 1946 for public action at the national level will not solve the problems of structural unemployment. Moreover, it takes more than a decision by the Federal Government to favor the award of defense contracts to labor-surplus areas to solve the economic problems of an anthractie mining county or an old textile city. As a result, the initiative and plans for such programs must be largely local or regional in character, and they are heavily dependent on the cooperation of business enterprises, labor unions, and civic groups, as well as local, state, and federal goverment agencies.

Once the volume of unemployment rises above a figure that represents usual turnover on jobs, its incidence changes among various groups in the labor force and its duration increases. For various combinations of reasons, including the incidence of layoffs, the hiring specifications for jobs in expanding industries or for replacements, and the transferability of the skills and experience of the unemployed, some workers secure new jobs more readily than others. Since cities do not have the same facilities as the nation for measuring monthly changes in the labor force and in unemployment, they are more dependent on measures of the character of unemployment as signals of economic distress. These signals are an increase in part-time employment, a mounting average duration of unemployment, and an increasing proportion of workers from certain industries, occupations, or age and racial groups among the unemployed. Even at the national level, changes in the incidence and duration of unemployment may be of greater significance as an index of economic welfare than changes in its *volume*, per se.

No stone should be left unturned that will minimize the social costs of labor-force adapations to short-term changes in the levels of employment and to longer-term changes in its distribution by industry and occupation. Unemployment, from whatever cause, bears heavily on urban workers, but, if prolonged, it has a self-generating quality that creates "unemployables." The social costs of unemployment to a community are seldom, if ever, negligible.

Minimizing unemployment or maximizing employment thus becomes a central objective both to agencies concerned with planning economic development in a community and to employers, unions, and placement and training officers engaged in labor-market operations. The Philadelphia area has the resources to meet the challenge of both short- and long-run changes in the economy. Because of its maturity as an industrial center, there is a relatively high proportion of obsolescent equipment in a few of its older industries. On the whole, however, the community has diversified and up-to-date manufacturing facilities, financial resources, technical know-how, and transportation and other business service facilities, as well as a skilled and experienced labor force that is relatively mobile with respect to occupation and industry and relatively stable with respect to job and residence attachments. The quality of the future labor force is assured by adequate training facilities at all levels of educational attainment. Moreover, the area's industrial relations record is "good" when compared with other metropolitan centers of comparable size and there have been outstanding examples of union-management cooperation to solve specific economic problems in local industries. Since Philadelphia's business and labor leaders are civic-minded and participate in a wide variety of educational and welfare programs in the community, the necessary rapport between leadership and community support has been established.

Counselling and placement services and extensive personnel programs in business establishments effectuate the daily round of job transactions that implement employment policy in the local labor market. Important steps toward maximizing the utilization of the labor force in the Philadelphia area have already been taken. Both public and private agencies have rendered excellent service in planning for economic development, and a municipal ordinance on fair employment practices has laid the groundwork for a policy that stresses employment in terms of qualifications for a job other than race or religion. The future utilization of the area's labor force depends upon the continued development of these and related activities and upon widespread community support to this end.

APPENDIX TABLES

Appendix Table 1

POPULATION OF THE UNITED STATES, URBAN UNITED STATES, AND FIVE LARGEST CITIES, BY DECADE 1880-1950

Year	United States	Urban United States	New York	Chicago	Philadel-phia	Los Angeles	Detroit
1880	50,155,783	14,129,735	1,911,698	503,185	847,170	11,183	116,340
1890	62,947,714	22,106,265	2,507,414	1,099,850	1,046,964	50,395	205,876
1900	75,994,575	30,159,921	3,437,202	1,698,575	1,293,697	102,479	285,704
1910	91,972,266	41,998,932	4,766,883	2,185,283	1,549,008	319,198	465,766
1920	105,710,620	54,157,973	5,620,048	2,701,705	1,823,779	576,673	993,678
1930	122,775,046	68,954,823	6,930,446	3,376,438	1,950,961	1,238,048	1,568,662
1940	131,669,275	74,423,702	7,454,995	3,396,808	1,931,334	1,504,277	1,623,452
1950	150,697,361	96,467,686	7,891,957	3,620,962	2,071,605	1,970,358	1,849,568

Sources: Data for 1880 to 1940 from *1940 Census of Population,* Vol. I, pp. 18, 32; data for 1950 from *1950 Census of Population,* Vol. II, part 1, *General Characteristics,* pp. 87, 140.

Appendix Table 2

PERCENTAGE CHANGES IN POPULATION OF THE UNITED STATES, URBAN UNITED STATES, AND FIVE LARGEST CITIES, BY DECADE 1880-1950

Year	United States	Urban United States	New York	Chicago	Phila-delphia	Los Angeles	Detroit
1880-1890	+25.5	+56.5	+31.2	+118.6	+23.6	+350.6	+ 77.0
1890-1900	+20.7	+36.4	+37.1	+ 54.4	+23.6	+103.4	+ 38.8
1900-1910	+21.0	+39.3	+38.7	+ 28.7	+19.7	+211.5	+ 63.0
1910-1920	+14.9	+29.0	+17.9	+ 23.6	+17.7	+ 80.7	+113.3
1920-1930	+16.1	+27.3	+23.3	+ 25.0	+ 7.0	+114.7	+ 57.9
1930-1940	+ 7.2	+ 7.9	+ 7.6	+ 0.6	− 1.0	+ 21.5	+ 3.5
1940-1950	+14.5	+29.6	+ 5.9	+ 6.6	+ 7.3	+ 31.0	+ 13.9

Source: Computed from Appendix Table 1.

Appendix Table 3

Estimated Annual Average Number of Manufacturing Wage Jobs in the United States and Five Industrial Areas,[a] in Selected Years, 1899-1947

(IN THOUSANDS)

Year	United States	New York	Chicago	Phila-delphia	Los Angeles	Detroit
1899	4,502	541	239	269	5	45
1904	5,182	663	267	290	10	59
1909	6,262	802	336	332	18	90
1914	6,476	848	375	336	25	131
1919	8,424	1,004	486	451	54	261
1921	6,475	811	375	335	50	163
1923	8,194	905	482	395	67	288
1925	7,871	852	472	353	73	298
1927	7,848	846	475	354	79	267
1929	8,370	888	526	368	100	291
1931	6,163	692	365	286	74	207
1933	5,788	601	321	256	67	202
1935	7,204	766	421	312	94	331
1937	8,569	848	539	346	129	407
1939	7,887	850	484	322	126	311
1939 (Revised)	7,808	843	478	321	125	311
1947	11,916	1,218	756	438	277	454

Sources: Data for the United States: for 1899 to 1939 from the *1939 Census of Manufactures, Vol. III, Reports for States and Outlying Areas,* Table 2, p. 19; for 1939 (revised) and 1947 from *1947 Census of Manufactures.* Data for Industrial Areas: from 1899 to 1927 are estimates made by the Industrial Research Department, based on figures published in Glenn E. McLaughlin, *Growth of American Manufacturing Areas* (University of Pittsburgh, 1938), Table 21, p. 98. McLaughlin's figures have been adjusted to exclude estimates of wage earners in those industries not covered by the Census of Manufactures in 1939. Data for 1929 to 1933 are from the published volumes of the Census of Manufactures for these years, as adjusted by the Industrial Research Department. Data for 1935 and 1937 are from the *Biennial Census of Manufactures, 1937,* Part 1. Data for 1939 are from the same volume as those for the United States, Table 2 for each state. Revised data for 1939 and for 1947 are from *1947 Census of Manufactures,* adjusted for comparable geographic coverage.

[a] The geographic definitions of the industrial areas in this table for all years (including 1947) are those used in the *1939 Census of Manufactures.* Data for years prior to 1939 have been adjusted so that the definition of what constitutes manufacturing is the same from 1899 through 1939; however, no attempt has been made to adjust for changes in the size of establishment covered, as measured by value of product. Figures for 1939 were revised by the Bureau of the Census to cover changes in the definition of manufacturing adopted in 1947; it has not been feasible to carry these revisions back through the entire period and therefore both sets of figures for 1939 are shown here.

Appendix Table 4

Rank Order of Manufacturing Industries with High Locational Quotients[a] in Philadelphia, 1950

(with corresponding quotient in the Philadelphia Standard Metropolitan Area)

Industry	City	Standard Metropolitan Area
Carpets, rugs, and other floor coverings	3.75	3.50
Leather: tanned, curried, and finished	3.67	2.67
Miscellaneous textile mill products	3.50	2.50
Tobacco manufacturers	3.00	2.17
Knitting mills	3.00	2.85
Confectionery and related products	2.60	2.00
Railroad and miscellaneous transportation equipment	2.50	3.00
Ship and boat building and repairing	2.27	2.82
Dyeing and finishing textiles, except knit goods	2.25	1.75
Paperboard containers and boxes	2.13	1.75
Apparel and accessories	1.94	1.55
Professional equipment and supplies	1.88	1.63
Electrical machinery, equipment, and supplies	1.50	1.54
Drugs and medicines	1.50	1.50
Paints, varnishes, and related products	1.50	1.50
Leather products, except footwear	1.50	1.25
Bakery products	1.47	1.11
Petroleum refining	1.44	2.28
Fabricated nonferrous metal products	1.43	1.14
Miscellaneous paper and pulp products	1.33	1.44
Miscellaneous fabricated textile products	1.33	1.00
Fabricated steel products	1.27	1.14
Miscellaneous food preparations and kindred products	1.25	1.00

Source: Computed from *1950 Census of Population, Detailed Characteristics,* pp. 1:283-84, 38: 441-42.

[a] Out of a possible 59 industries in the Census of Population Code, excluding "not specified manufacturing." When measured by data from the *1947 Census of Manufactures* a comparable listing shows 25 industries out of a possible 56. There is one industry segment (Miscellaneous nonmetallic mineral and stone products) with a quotient above 1.25 in the Standard Metropolitan Area but not in the city.

Appendix Table 5

ESTIMATED AVERAGE ANNUAL EMPLOYMENT OF FACTORY WAGE EARNERS BY INDUSTRY GROUP IN PHILADELPHIA COUNTY AND THE PHILADELPHIA FIVE-COUNTY AREA

1919-1950

(IN THOUSANDS)

PHILADELPHIA COUNTY

Industry group[a]	1919	1920	1921	1922	1923	1924	1925	1926	1927	1928	1929
All industries	262	266	221	240	253	237	235	238	236	236	244
Durable goods industries	96	100	68	78	88	79	79	80	73	73	75
Lumber & timber products	2	2	1	2	1	2	2	2	2	1	1
Furniture	6	5	5	5	6	5	6	5	6	5	5
Stone, clay, & glass products	3	4	3	3	4	3	4	4	4	4	4
Iron & steel products	21	22	13	14	14	13	14	17	13	13	13
Nonferrous metal products	5	6	5	6	6	6	6	5	6	5	5
Electrical machinery	5	8	8	6	7	10	11	10	11	14	16
Machinery, exc. electrical	16	16	10	14	16	13	10	11	11	12	13
Automobiles & auto. equip.	8	8	4	7	10	8	9	10	5	6	8
Trans. equip., exc. auto.	20	19	11	13	15	10	9	8	6	5	2
Miscellaneous manufacturing	10	10	8	8	9	9	8	8	9	8	8
Nondurable goods industries	166	166	153	162	165	158	156	158	163	163	169
Food & kindred products	19	20	18	18	18	18	18	19	17	18	18
Tobacco manufactures	6	7	7	7	8	7	8	8	8	9	9
Textile mill products	64	63	62	69	71	66	67	64	65	63	62
Apparel & related products	24	26	23	23	21	22	19	20	28	30	32
Paper & allied products	9	8	7	8	9	9	8	9	8	7	7
Printing, publishing, & allied products	14	14	13	13	13	13	13	14	15	16	17
Chemicals & allied products	10	10	8	8	8	8	8	8	8	7	8
Petroleum & coal products	7	6	4	6	6	5	5	5	4	3	6
Rubber products	1	1	1	*	1	1	1	1	*	1	*
Leather & leather products	12	11	10	10	10	9	9	10	10	9	10

See footnotes at end of table.

Appendix Table 5
(CONTINUED)
PHILADELPHIA COUNTY

Industry group[a]	1930	1931	1932	1933	1934	1935	1936	1937	1938	1939	1940
All industries	222	197	173	191	204	215	228	234	205	216	227
Durable goods industries	63	51	40	44	50	55	65	68	55	61	73
Lumber & timber products	1	1	1	1	*	1	1	1	1	1	1
Furniture	5	4	3	4	4	4	5	5	5	5	5
Stone, clay, & glass products	3	2	1	1	2	2	2	3	2	2	3
Iron & steel products	12	10	7	7	8	9	11	13	11	14	16
Nonferrous metal products	5	4	3	3	3	3	4	4	4	4	5
Electrical machinery	12	10	8	10	12	14	17	14	9	9	11
Machinery, exc. electrical	10	8	6	6	8	8	10	12	10	10	13
Automobiles & auto. equip.	5	4	3	4	4	6	8	8	6	8	10
Trans. equip., exc. auto.	2	1	1	1	2	1	*	*	*	*	1
Miscellaneous manufacturing	8	7	7	7	7	7	7	8	7	8	8
Nondurable goods industries	159	146	133	147	154	160	163	166	150	155	154
Food & kindred products	19	19	18	22	24	22	23	23	22	22	22
Tobacco manufactures	8	7	6	6	7	7	8	8	8	8	8
Textile mill products	55	48	43	48	47	52	50	50	41	42	40
Apparel & related products	31	29	27	28	31	33	35	36	34	36	38
Paper & allied products	7	6	6	7	7	8	8	7	7	8	8
Printing, publishing, & allied products	17	15	14	14	14	14	15	17	16	16	16
Chemicals & allied products	7	8	7	7	8	8	8	9	8	8	8
Petroleum & coal products	5	5	5	6	7	6	7	7	6	6	4
Rubber products	1	1	*	1	1	1	1	1	1	1	2
Leather & leather products	9	8	7	8	8	9	8	8	7	8	8

See footnotes at end of table.

Appendix Table 5
(CONTINUED)
PHILADELPHIA COUNTY

Industry group[a]	1941	1942	1943	1944	1945	1946	1947	1948	1949	1950
All industries	264	278	297	288	271	282	285	285	263	268
Durable goods industries	98	119	139	134	111	106	108	106	93	98
Lumber & timber products	1	1	1	1	1	1	1	1	1	1
Furniture	5	5	4	5	5	6	5	6	5	5
Stone, clay, & glass products	3	4	3	3	3	4	3	3	3	3
Iron & steel products	21	24	28	24	25	20	20	19	16	17
Nonferrous metal products	7	7	8	7	11	9	11	11	9	12
Electrical machinery	16	19	22	21	16	19	19	20	18	19
Machinery, exc. electrical	18	22	25	25	20	20	22	22	17	17
Automobiles & auto. equip.	12	11	2	2	2	12	11	9	10	10
Trans. equip., exc. auto.	5	16	35	34	16	3	3	3	3	2
Miscellaneous manufacturing	10	10	11	12	12	12	13	12	11	12
Nondurable goods industries	166	159	158	154	160	176	177	179	170	170
Food & kindred products	23	22	24	24	24	27	26	26	26	26
Tobacco manufactures	9	8	8	7	7	7	7	7	6	6
Textile mill products	42	39	36	34	36	40	40	41	37	38
Apparel & related products	41	40	40	39	39	42	44	47	46	45
Paper & allied products	9	8	9	9	10	11	10	9	9	9
Printing, publishing, & allied products	17	17	16	16	18	21	22	20	20	20
Chemicals & allied products	10	10	11	12	12	12	11	12	10	10
Petroleum & coal products	5	5	5	5	6	6	7	7	6	6
Rubber products	2	2	2	2	1	2	2	2	2	2
Leather & leather products	8	8	7	6	7	8	8	8	8	8

See footnotes at end of table.

Appendix Table 5
(CONTINUED)
PHILADELPHIA FIVE-COUNTY AREA

Industry group[a]	1919	1920	1921	1922	1923	1924	1925	1926	1927	1928	1929
All industries	383	368	291	315	336	306	308	313	314	313	328
Durable goods industries	183	165	102	111	129	111	112	119	113	111	119
Lumber & timber products	3	2	2	3	2	3	3	3	3	2	2
Furniture	7	6	6	6	7	6	7	6	8	7	6
Stone, clay, & glass products	5	7	6	7	8	7	8	8	8	8	8
Iron & steel products	42	45	27	31	37	30	31	34	29	30	30
Nonferrous metal products	6	6	6	7	8	8	8	7	7	6	6
Electrical machinery	5	8	7	6	7	10	11	11	11	14	16
Machinery, exc. electrical	20	19	12	15	18	14	12	12	15	15	17
Automobiles & auto. equip.	9	10	5	9	12	10	11	12	7	7	14
Trans. equip., exc. auto.	76	50	22	17	20	13	12	17	15	13	10
Miscellaneous manufacturing	10	12	9	10	10	10	9	9	10	9	10
Nondurable goods industries	200	203	189	204	207	195	196	194	201	202	209
Food & kindred products	21	22	20	20	20	21	21	21	20	20	21
Tobacco manufactures	10	12	12	12	12	10	10	10	10	10	10
Textile mill products	82	82	82	93	94	87	90	85	86	84	83
Apparel & related products	27	28	26	26	25	25	23	24	32	34	37
Paper & allied products	11	11	10	10	11	11	12	12	11	10	10
Printing, publishing, & allied products	15	15	13	13	13	13	14	15	15	17	18
Chemicals & allied products	13	12	9	11	11	10	9	9	9	9	9
Petroleum & coal products	7	7	5	7	7	6	5	7	6	5	9
Rubber products	2	2	2	1	2	2	2	1	1	2	2
Leather & leather products	12	12	10	11	12	10	10	10	11	11	10

See footnotes at end of table.

Appendix Table 5
(CONTINUED)
PHILADELPHIA FIVE-COUNTY AREA

Industry group[a]	1930	1931	1932	1933	1934	1935	1936	1937	1938	1939	1940
All industries	304	265	233	258	277	293	312	326	284	301	323
Durable goods industries	107	83	62	70	78	85	104	113	91	101	121
Lumber & timber products	2	1	1	1	1	1	1	1	1	1	1
Furniture	6	5	4	5	5	5	6	6	5	5	6
Stone, clay, & glass products	6	5	4	4	5	5	6	7	6	7	7
Iron & steel products	29	21	16	18	20	21	26	31	24	27	33
Nonferrous metal products	7	5	4	4	4	5	5	6	5	6	7
Electrical machinery	12	11	7	10	12	14	17	14	9	9	11
Machinery, exc. electrical	14	11	8	9	11	12	15	18	15	15	19
Automobiles & auto. equip.	11	8	6	7	8	10	12	12	10	11	14
Trans. equip., exc. auto.	11	8	4	4	4	4	7	8	7	10	12
Miscellaneous manufacturing	9	8	8	8	8	8	9	10	9	10	11
Nondurable goods industries	197	182	171	188	199	208	208	213	193	200	202
Food & kindred products	21	22	21	25	26	26	26	26	25	26	26
Tobacco manufactures	9	8	6	6	7	7	8	9	8	8	8
Textile mill products	76	67	64	71	71	79	74	73	62	62	61
Apparel & related products	36	34	32	34	37	39	42	44	42	44	47
Paper & allied products	10	9	9	10	11	11	11	12	11	13	13
Printing, publishing, & allied products	17	15	14	15	15	15	16	17	17	17	17
Chemicals & allied products	8	9	8	9	10	10	10	11	9	10	11
Petroleum & coal products	8	8	8	9	11	10	10	10	9	8	7
Rubber products	2	1	1	1	2	2	2	2	2	3	3
Leather & leather products	10	9	8	8	9	9	9	9	8	9	9

See footnotes at end of table.

Appendix Table 5
(CONCLUDED)
PHILADELPHIA FIVE-COUNTY AREA

Industry group[a]	1941	1942	1943	1944	1945	1946	1947	1948	1949	1950
All industries	384	424	458	443	410	408	405	410	384	391
Durable goods industries	163	215	255	242	202	179	174	174	156	161
Lumber & timber products	1	1	1	1	1	1	1	2	1	1
Furniture	6	6	5	6	6	8	7	7	7	8
Stone, clay, & glass products	9	9	8	7	7	8	8	9	8	9
Iron & steel products	44	50	52	47	46	40	42	40	35	38
Nonferrous metal products	10	10	11	10	14	13	14	15	12	15
Electrical machinery	16	20	24	24	19	21	21	23	22	24
Machinery, exc. electrical	26	34	40	41	33	30	32	33	27	28
Automobiles & auto. equip.	17	15	6	6	7	19	17	15	14	15
Trans. equip., exc. auto.	21	56	93	84	53	22	15	15	17	9
Miscellaneous manufacturing	13	14	15	16	16	17	17	15	13	14
Nondurable goods industries	221	209	203	201	208	229	231	236	228	230
Food & kindred products	28	27	28	30	31	34	32	32	31	31
Tobacco manufactures	9	8	8	7	7	7	8	8	6	6
Textile mill products	66	59	53	51	53	60	61	62	58	59
Apparel & related products	51	50	48	47	47	50	53	55	56	56
Paper & allied products	16	14	14	14	15	17	16	15	15	16
Printing, publishing, & allied products	18	17	17	17	19	22	23	22	22	22
Chemicals & allied products	12	14	16	16	16	16	15	15	15	15
Petroleum & coal products	8	8	8	8	9	10	10	11	10	10
Rubber products	4	3	3	4	3	4	4	7	7	6
Leather & leather products	9	9	8	7	8	9	9	9	8	9

Source: Pennsylvania Department of Internal Affairs, *Reports on Productive Industries, 1919-1941*, supplemented by *Industrial Directories of Pennsylvania* and unpublished tabulations.

[a] The original data from the Department of Internal Affairs have been converted to the classifications used in the Census of Manufactures of 1939, and adjusted for unallocated items by reference to directories.

* Starred items are those in which fewer than 500 persons were reported.

Appendix Table 6
Employment Relative to Population by Industry Group Philadelphia and the United States 1910 and 1950

Industry group	Philadelphia: Employed per 10,000 population 1910	Philadelphia: Employed per 10,000 population 1950	Philadelphia: Percentage change 1910-1950	United States: Employed per 10,000 nonfarm population 1910	United States: Employed per 10,000 nonfarm population 1950	United States: Percentage change 1910-1950
All industries	4,415	3,995	- 9.5	4,105	3,875	- 5.6
Manufacturing	1,743	1,427	- 18.1	1,215	1,164	- 4.2
Food and kindred products	94	133	+ 41.5	81	112	+ 38.3
Tobacco manufacturers	36	25	- 30.6	31	8	- 74.2
Textile mill products	403	180	- 55.3	145	104	- 28.3
Apparel and accessories	224	199	- 11.2	98	80	- 18.4
Lumber and wood products, etc.	58	34	- 41.4	149	95	- 36.2
Paper and allied products	37	49	+ 32.4	21	37	+ 76.2
Printing, publishing, etc.	114	104	- 8.8	63	69	+ 9.5
Chemicals, etc.	57	96	+ 68.4	30	76	+153.3
Leather and leather products	72	35	- 51.4	56	31	- 44.6
Metal industries, etc.	432	487	+ 12.7	326	450	+ 38.0
Other manufacturing	216	85	- 60.6	215	102	- 52.6
Nonmanufacturing	2,672	2,568	- 3.9	2,890	2,711	- 6.2
Extractive industries	45	11	- 75.6	182	84	- 53.8
Construction	295	227	- 23.1	364	274	- 24.7
Transportation, communications, and other public utilities	413	341	- 17.4	514	348	- 32.3
Transportation	347	243	- 30.0	443	234	- 47.2
Telecommunications, utilities, and sanitary services	66	98	+ 48.5	71	114	+ 60.6
Wholesale and retail trade	820	869	+ 6.0	696	843	+ 21.1
Finance, insurance, etc.	110	176	+ 60.0	98	153	+ 56.1
Business and repair services	32	102	+218.8	46	113	+145.7
Personal services	590	284	- 51.9	583	279	- 52.1
Entertainment, etc.	31	33	+ 6.5	29	44	+ 51.7
Professional and related services	219	324	+ 47.9	280	374	+ 33.6
Public administration	117	201	+ 71.8	98	199	+103.1

Source: Computed from Technical Appendix Table A, using population data from Decennial Censuses of Population, except for the nonfarm population in 1910. This population base is derived from Leon Truesdell, *Farm Population of the United States* (Census Monograph VI, 1926), Tables 8 and 9.

Appendix Table 7

Percentage Distribution of Employment by Industry Group and Sex Philadelphia and the United States 1910 and 1950

Industry group	Philadelphia						United States					
	1910			1950			1910			1950		
	Total	Men	Women	Total	Men	Women	Total	Men	Women	Total	Men	Women
All Industries	100.0	100.0	100.0	100.0	100.0	100.0	100.0	100.0	100.0	100.0	100.0	100.0
Manufacturing	39.5	40.7	36.4	35.7	36.5	34.2	29.6	32.1	22.0	30.0	32.4	24.6
Food and kindred products	2.1	2.5	1.1	3.3	3.6	2.7	2.0	2.3	1.0	2.9	3.2	2.2
Tobacco manufactures	0.8	0.6	1.3	0.6	0.2	1.5	0.8	0.6	1.3	0.2	0.1	0.3
Textile mill products	9.2	6.5	15.7	4.5	3.6	6.3	3.5	2.5	6.7	2.7	2.2	3.9
Apparel and accessories	5.1	4.0	7.8	5.0	2.9	9.2	2.4	1.7	4.5	2.1	0.9	4.8
Lumber and wood products, etc.	1.3	1.7	0.2	0.9	1.1	0.3	3.6	4.7	0.4	2.4	3.3	0.6
Paper and allied products	0.8	0.7	1.3	1.2	1.2	1.2	0.5	0.5	0.6	1.0	1.0	0.7
Printing, publishing, etc.	2.6	2.8	2.1	2.6	2.9	2.1	1.5	1.6	1.3	1.8	1.9	1.4
Chemicals, etc.	1.3	1.5	0.9	2.4	2.9	1.5	0.7	0.8	0.4	1.9	2.3	1.1
Leather and leather products	1.6	1.9	1.1	0.9	0.9	0.8	1.4	1.4	1.3	0.8	0.6	1.2
Metal industries, etc.	9.8	13.0	1.6	12.2	15.1	6.5	8.0	9.9	1.8	11.6	14.1	6.1
Other manufacturing	4.9	5.5	3.3	2.1	2.1	2.1	5.2	6.1	2.7	2.6	2.8	2.3
Nonmanufacturing	60.5	59.3	63.6	64.3	63.5	65.8	70.4	67.9	78.0	70.0	67.6	75.4
Extractive industries	1.0	1.4	0.1	0.3	0.4	0.1	4.4	5.9	0.1	2.2	3.0	0.2
Construction	6.7	9.2	0.2	5.7	8.2	0.6	8.9	11.7	0.1	7.1	9.9	0.7
Transportation, communications, and other public utilities	9.4	12.5	1.5	8.5	10.6	4.4	12.5	15.8	2.2	9.0	10.9	4.6
Transportation	7.9	10.9	0.3	6.1	8.4	1.5	10.8	14.1	0.5	6.1	8.1	1.3
Telecommunications, utilities, and sanitary services	1.5	1.6	1.2	2.4	2.2	2.9	1.7	1.7	1.7	2.9	2.8	3.3
Wholesale and retail trade	18.6	20.1	14.8	21.8	22.0	21.4	17.0	18.1	13.4	21.8	20.8	24.0
Finance, insurance, etc.	2.5	2.8	1.6	4.4	3.6	5.9	2.4	2.7	1.3	4.0	3.4	5.3
Business and repair services	0.7	1.0	0.0	2.6	3.2	1.2	1.1	1.5	0.0	2.9	3.7	1.2
Personal services	13.3	4.1	36.7	7.1	3.6	14.2	14.2	3.7	46.4	7.2	3.4	15.7
Entertainment, etc.	0.7	0.8	0.5	0.8	0.9	0.7	0.7	0.8	0.6	1.1	1.2	1.0
Professional and related services	5.0	3.9	7.7	8.1	5.1	14.1	6.8	4.8	13.1	9.6	5.8	18.3
Public administration	2.6	3.5	0.5	5.0	5.9	3.2	2.4	2.9	0.8	5.1	5.5	4.4

Source: Computed from Technical Appendix Table A.

Appendix Table 8

Percentage Distribution, Percentage of the United States, and Locational Quotients of Employment by Industry Group Philadelphia City and Standard Metropolitan Area, 1950

Industry group	City			Standard Metropolitan Area		
	Percentage distribution	Percentage of U.S.	Locational quotient	Percentage distribution	Percentage of U.S.	Locational quotient
Total employed in nonagricultural industries[a]	100.0	1.7	1.00	100.0	2.9	1.00
Manufacturing	35.8	2.0	1.19	37.9	3.6	1.26
Durable goods	14.5	1.5	0.91	16.6	3.0	1.04
Lumber and wood products, furniture and fixtures	0.8	0.6	0.33	0.8	0.9	0.33
Stone, clay, and glass products	0.5	0.8	0.50	0.8	2.5	0.80
Metal industries	3.9	1.6	0.95	4.9	3.4	1.20
Machinery, except electrical	2.5	1.5	0.93	2.4	2.6	0.89
Electrical machinery, equipment, and supplies	2.9	3.0	1.81	3.2	5.6	2.00
Transportation equipment	2.4	1.4	0.86	2.9	3.0	1.04
Professional and photographic equipment, and watches	0.6	2.3	1.50	0.6	3.8	1.50
Miscellaneous manufacturing industries	0.9	1.6	0.90	1.0	3.1	1.00
Nondurable goods	20.9	2.5	1.51	20.9	4.3	1.51
Food and kindred products	3.3	1.9	1.14	3.1	3.1	1.07
Tobacco manufactures	0.6	5.4	3.00	0.5	7.0	2.50
Textile mill products	4.6	3.0	1.84	4.5	5.0	1.80
Apparel and other fabricated textile products	5.0	3.8	2.27	4.2	5.4	1.91
Paper and allied products	1.2	2.1	1.20	1.4	4.2	1.40
Printing, publishing, and allied industries	2.6	2.5	1.44	2.5	4.0	1.39
Chemicals and allied products	1.4	1.8	1.08	1.9	4.1	1.46
Petroleum and coal products	1.0	2.7	1.67	1.6	8.0	2.67
Rubber products	0.3	1.0	0.60	0.5	3.0	1.00
Leather and leather products	0.9	1.9	1.13	0.7	2.6	0.88
Not specified manufacturing industries	0.4	3.0	2.00	0.4	4.5	2.00
Nonmanufacturing	64.2	1.5	0.92	62.1	2.5	0.89
Extractive industries, except agriculture	0.1	0.0	0.05	0.1	0.2	0.05
Construction	5.7	1.3	0.80	6.4	2.6	0.90
Transportation, communications, and other public utilities	8.6	1.6	0.96	8.2	2.6	0.91
Transportation	6.1	1.7	1.00	5.5	2.6	0.90
Telecommunications, utilities, and sanitary services	2.5	1.4	0.86	2.7	2.6	0.93
Wholesale and retail trade	21.8	1.7	1.00	20.0	2.6	0.92
Finance, insurance, and real estate	4.4	1.9	1.10	4.5	3.2	1.13
Business and repair services	2.6	1.5	0.90	2.6	2.5	0.90
Personal services	7.1	1.7	0.99	6.4	2.5	0.89
Entertainment and recreational services	0.8	1.2	0.73	0.8	2.0	0.73
Professional and related services	8.1	1.4	0.84	8.7	2.6	0.91
Public administration	5.0	1.6	0.98	4.4	2.4	0.86

Source: Computed from *1950 Census of Population, Detailed Characteristics*, pp. 1:283-84, 38:441-42.

[a] Excluding persons for whom industry was not reported.

Appendix Table 9

Percentage Distribution of Foreign-born White Population from Each Principal Country of Origin, Philadelphia, by Decade, 1900-1950

	1900	1910	1920	1930	1940	1950
Total population	1,293,697	1,549,008	1,823,779	1,950,961	1,931,334	2,071,605
Foreign-born whites	295,340	384,707	400,744	368,624	290,325	232,587
	100.0	100.0	100.0	100.0	100.0	100.0
Northern Europe	49.3	34.1	26.6	24.6	21.9	19.4
England and Wales	12.4	9.5	7.7	6.8	6.0	5.5
Scotland	2.9	2.4	2.1	3.1	2.8	2.7
Ireland	33.3	21.6	16.1	14.1	12.5	10.7
Sweden	0.7	0.6	0.7	0.6	0.6	0.5
Central Europe	30.4	28.7	25.5	25.3	25.1	25.4
France	0.9	0.7	1.0	0.8	0.7	0.8
Germany	24.2	15.2	9.9	10.3	9.4	8.5
Poland	2.6	6.6	7.8	8.3	8.2	8.7
Czechoslovakia	—	—	0.6	1.1	0.7	0.9
Austria	1.8	3.0	3.3	2.9	3.6	3.7
Hungary	0.9	3.2	2.9	1.9	2.5	2.8
Eastern & Southern Europe	16.2	33.0	42.3	44.4	47.2	47.7
Russia and Lithuania	9.8	20.0	25.0	23.8	24.9	25.2
Rumania	0.4	1.2	1.4	2.1	2.0	1.6
Italy	6.0	11.8	15.9	18.5	20.3	20.9
Canada	1.1	1.0	1.0	1.2	1.2	1.6
All other countries	3.0	3.2	4.6	4.5	4.6	5.9

Sources: Data for 1900, 1910, and 1920 from *1920 Census of Population,* Vol. II, p. 761 (adjusted to add to 100.0); data for 1930 computed from *1930 Census of Population,* Vol. II, p. 832; data for 1940 computed from *1940 Census of Population,* Vol. II, Part 1, p. 156; data for 1950 computed from *1950 Census of Population, General Characteristics,* p. 38:121.

Appendix Table 10

Population and Labor Force, 14 Years of Age and Over, by Sex for Philadelphia, Philadelphia Standard Metropolitan Area, and the United States by Decade 1910-1950 (in thousands)

Year	Philadelphia				Philadelphia Standard Metropolitan Area				United States			
	Total population 14 years of age and over	Labor Force			Total population 14 years of age and over	Labor Force			Total population 14 years of age and over	Labor Force		
		Total	Men	Women		Total	Men	Women		Total	Men	Women
1910	1,157	710	510	200	n.a.	n.a.	n.a.	n.a.	64,321	36,688	29,406	7,282
1920	1,352	819	603	216	1,999	n.a.	n.a.	n.a.	74,144	41,236	32,806	8,430
1930	1,497	889	641	248	2,371	1,365	1,008	357	89,101	47,404	37,008	10,396
1940	1,558	884	612	272	2,561	1,419	1,008	411	101,103	53,299	40,284	13,015
1950	1,631	891	603	288	2,849	1,550	1,085	465	112,354	60,054	43,553	16,501

Sources: *For Philadelphia:* Population data are as published in Censuses of Population. Labor-force data for 1910 and 1920 are unadjusted "gainful worker" figures which because of the relative prosperity of the period are assumed to be a close approximation of the labor force at those dates; data for 1930 are "gainful worker" figures adjusted to conform to the Durand-Goldfield "Estimates of Labor Force, Employment and Unemployment in the United States 1940 and 1930" *(1940 Census of Population);* for 1940, Census data have been adjusted for persons not reporting work status; data for 1950 are from the *1950 Census of Population, General Characteristics.*

For the Philadelphia Standard Metropolitan Area: Population data for 1910 are not available; for 1920 to 1950, data are from Censuses of Population. Labor-force data for 1910 and 1920 are not available; for 1930, data are "gainful worker" figures from *1930 Census of Population* (requisite information for adjustment not available); for 1940, census data have been adjusted for persons not reporting work status; for 1950, data are from the *1950 Census of Population, General Characteristics.*

For the United States: Population data are as published in Censuses of Population. Labor-force data for 1910 are adjusted for the overcount of agricultural workers in that year; data for 1920 are from *1920 Census of Population;* data for 1930 and 1940 are from the Durand-Goldfield publication cited above; data for 1950 are from the *1950 Census of Population, General Characteristics.*

Appendix Table 11

Age and Sex of the Labor Force and the Population, Philadelphia and the United States 1910 and 1950 (in thousands)

Age	1910						1950					
	Philadelphia			United States			Philadelphia			United States		
	Total	Men	Women	Total	Men	Women	Total	Men	Women	Total	Men	Women
Labor force												
Total 14 years of age and over	710	510	200	36,688	29,406	7,282	889	601	288	59,643	43,091	16,552
14-20	129	70	59	6,091	4,293	1,798	67	33	34	5,318	3,343	1,975
21-44	421	310	111	21,530	17,233	4,297	504	335	169	33,774	24,114	9,660
45-64	132	109	23	7,624	6,611	1,013	277	201	76	17,664	13,254	4,410
65 and over	28	21	7	1,443	1,269	174	41	32	9	2,887	2,380	507
Median age	33.9	35.3	29.9	34.7	35.5	31.3	39.0	40.2	36.6	38.4	39.1	36.7
Population												
Total 14 years of age and over	1,157	564	593	64,321	33,362	30,959	1,624	772	852	111,703	54,601	57,102
14-20	200	96	104	12,799	6,384	6,415	185	89	96	14,971	7,464	7,507
21-44	645	319	326	34,102	17,797	16,305	796	379	417	54,130	26,378	27,752
45-64	249	122	127	13,460	7,188	6,272	470	229	241	30,345	15,025	15,320
65 and over	63	27	36	3,960	1,993	1,967	173	75	98	12,257	5,734	6,523
Median age	35.1	35.0	35.2	34.6	34.9	34.3	39.9	39.8	40.0	39.1	39.0	39.2

Sources: From 1910 and 1950 Censuses of Population. Labor force in 1910 refers to gainful workers. For 1910, estimates of the age distribution and an adjustment for the overcount of agricultural workers in the United States have been made. The methodology and data for these adjustments are from A. M. Edwards, *Comparative Occupation Statistics for the United States, 1870 to 1940* (1940 Census Monograph). Data for 1950 are based on a 20 per cent sample and therefore do not agree with totals from the complete count used in Appendix Table 10.

Appendix Table 12

OCCUPATION GROUP OF GAINFUL WORKERS IN 1910 AND OF THE EXPERIENCED CIVILIAN LABOR FORCE IN 1950
14 YEARS OF AGE AND OVER, BY SEX
PHILADELPHIA AND THE UNITED STATES

(IN THOUSANDS)

Occupation group	Men 1910	Men 1950	Women 1910	Women 1950	Percentage change 1910-1950 Men	Percentage change 1910-1950 Women
			Philadelphia			
All occupations	509	595	200	288	+16.9	+ 44.0
Professional, technical, and kindred workers	23	44	13	27	+91.3	+107.7
Managers, officials, and proprietors	59	60	9	9	+ 1.7	0.0
Clerical and kindred workers	52	55	24	82	+ 5.8	+241.7
Sales workers	34	44	10	20	+29.4	+100.0
Craftsmen, foremen, and kindred workers	120	129	5	6	+ 7.5	+ 20.0
Operatives and kindred workers	109	157	77	86	+44.0	+ 11.7
Service workers	35	54	60	56	+54.3	– 6.7
Laborers	77	52	2	2	–32.5	0.0
			United States[a]			
All occupations	19,372	36,303	6,233	15,861	+ 87.4	+154.5
Professional, technical, and kindred workers	961	3,024	724	1,964	+214.7	+171.3
Managers, officials, and proprietors	2,278	4,392	241	685	+ 92.8	+184.2
Clerical and kindred workers	1,318	2,679	692	4,392	+103.3	+534.7
Sales workers	1,477	2,666	390	1,378	+ 80.5	+253.3
Craftsmen, foremen, and kindred workers	4,224	7,907	111	245	+ 87.2	+120.7
Operatives and kindred workers	3,707	9,441	1,591	3,640	+154.7	+128.8
Service workers	1,123	2,582	2,378	3,418	+129.9	+ 43.7
Laborers	4,284	3,612	106	139	– 15.7	+ 31.1

Source: Data for 1910 are converted to the classifications used in 1950; data for 1950 from *1950 Census of Population, Detailed Characteristics,* pp. 1:261-62, 38:334-39. Persons for whom an occupation was not reported in 1950 are allocated to "Operatives and kindred workers" for comparability with data for 1910.

[a] Data for the United States are for nonfarm occupations only.

Appendix Table 13

Percentage Distribution of Employment by Occupation Group and Sex Philadelphia and the United States 1910 and 1950

Occupation group	1910 Total	1910 Men	1910 Women	1950 Total	1950 Men	1950 Women
	Philadelphia					
All occupations	100.0	100.0	100.0	100.0	100.0	100.0
Professional, technical, and kindred workers	5.1	4.5	6.7	8.4	7.8	9.7
Managers, officials, and proprietors	9.7	11.8	4.4	8.1	10.7	3.1
Clerical and kindred workers	10.8	10.3	12.3	16.2	9.6	29.4
Sales workers	6.2	6.6	5.1	7.4	7.7	6.9
Craftsmen, foremen, and kindred workers	17.4	23.4	2.4	15.4	21.9	2.1
Operatives and kindred workers	26.2	21.4	38.4	26.1	24.8	28.7
Service workers	13.6	7.0	30.0	12.6	9.2	19.3
Laborers	11.0	15.0	0.7	5.8	8.3	0.8
	United States					
All nonfarm occupations	100.0	100.0	100.0	100.0	100.0	100.0
Professional, technical, and kindred workers	6.7	5.1	11.6	9.9	8.6	12.8
Managers, officials, and proprietors	10.2	12.2	3.9	10.2	12.6	4.5
Clerical and kindred workers	7.9	6.9	11.1	13.9	7.6	28.3
Sales workers	7.4	7.8	6.3	7.9	7.6	8.8
Craftsmen, foremen, and kindred workers	16.8	21.7	1.8	15.7	21.9	1.6
Operatives and kindred workers	20.4	18.8	25.5	24.0	25.0	21.8
Service workers	13.8	5.8	38.2	11.5	7.1	21.4
Laborers	16.8	21.7	1.6	6.9	9.6	0.8

Source: Computed from Technical Appendix Table B.

Appendix Table 14

Employment Relative to Population by Occupation Group Philadelphia and the United States 1910 and 1950

Occupation group	Philadelphia		
	Employed per 10,000 population		Percentage change
	1910	1950	1910-1950
All occupations	4,415	3,995	- 9.5
Professional, technical, and kindred workers	226	336	+48.7
Managers, officials, and proprietors	428	326	-23.8
Clerical and kindred workers	478	647	+35.4
Sales workers	274	297	+ 8.4
Craftsmen, foremen, and kindred workers	769	613	-20.3
Operatives and kindred workers	1,157	1,042	- 9.9
Service workers	598	502	-16.1
Laborers	485	232	-52.2
	United States		
	Employed per 10,000 nonfarm population		Percentage change
	1910	1950	1910-1950
All nonfarm occupations	4,106	3,888	- 5.3
Professional, technical, and kindred workers	274	386	+40.9
Managers, officials, and proprietors	417	394	- 5.5
Clerical and kindred workers	326	542	+66.3
Sales workers	305	308	+ 1.0
Craftsmen, foremen, and kindred workers	691	610	-11.7
Operatives and kindred workers	838	933	+11.3
Service workers	566	447	-21.0
Laborers	689	268	-61.1

Source: Computed from Technical Appendix Table B. For source of population data see Appendix Table 6.

Appendix Table 15

Percentage Distribution of the Philadelphia Labor Force by Employment Status 1929-1938, 1940, 1943-1947, 1950

Date	Labor force	Total employed	Employed full time[a]	Employed part time[b]	Unemployed[c]
April 1929	100.0	91.5	86.0	5.5	8.5
April 1930	100.0	86.9	80.3	6.6	13.1[d]
April 1931	100.0	76.4	61.0	15.4	23.6
May 1932	100.0	59.3	37.1	22.2	40.7
April 1933	100.0	55.2	34.1	21.1	44.8
February 1934	100.0	63.9	49.0	14.9	36.1
May 1935	100.0	67.1	52.7	14.4	32.9
May 1936	100.0	70.2	60.3	9.9	29.8
May 1937	100.0	75.8	70.0	5.8	24.2
July-August 1938	100.0	67.6	61.0	6.6	32.4
March 1940	100.0	80.3	73.0	7.3	19.7
May 1943	100.0	97.1	91.6	5.5	2.9
May 1944	100.0	97.1	94.2	2.9	2.9
May 1945	100.0	98.2	89.8	8.4	1.8
October 1946	100.0	93.2	82.5	10.7	6.8
April 1947[e]	100.0	93.5	81.1	12.4	6.5
April 1950	100.0	93.4	85.9	7.5	6.6

Sources: Data for 1929 to 1938 from Industrial Research Department sample surveys. These figures differ slightly from previously published data, since they have been adjusted to conform more closely with labor-force concepts of 1940 and later. Data for 1940 from *1940 Census of Population.* Data for 1943 and 1944 from sample surveys conducted by the Bureau of the Census in cooperation with the Industrial Research Department. These figures have been revised from previously published data to conform to revisions made by the Bureau of the Census in the *Monthly Report on the Labor Force,* starting in July 1945. Data for 1945 from unpublished tabulations made by the Bureau of the Census, revised in the same manner as for 1943 and 1944. Data for 1946 to 1950 from Census Bureau Series P-LF, No. 1; P-51, No. 12; and PC-5, No. 36.

[a] The distribution between full-time and part-time workers was estimated for 1929. For 1930 to 1934, full-time work was defined as the customary hours of work in the industry. For 1935 to 1945, full-time work is 30 or more hours per week. For 1940, it was assumed that self-employed persons worked full time and unpaid family workers worked part time. For 1946 to 1950 full-time work is 35 or more hours per week.

[b] Includes persons with a job but not at work during Survey week from 1940 to 1950.

[c] Includes relief and emergency workers, 1930 to 1940, and persons willing and able to work but not actively seeking work as well as active job seekers from 1929 to 1938.

[d] Adjusted Census of Population data for 1930 indicate an unemployment rate of 9.7 per cent.

[e] Data refer to Philadelphia Metropolitan District.

Appendix Table 16

Estimated Average Annual Unemployment in the United States 1929-1950

Year	Civilian labor force[a] (in 000's)	Unemployed		
		Number (in 000's)	Per cent of civilian labor force	Per cent of nonagricultural labor force
1929	49,180	1,550	3.2	4.0
1930	49,820	4,340	8.7	11.0
1931	50,420	8,020	15.9	20.0
1932	51,000	12,060	23.6	29.5
1933	51,590	12,830	24.9	30.9
1934	52,230	11,340	21.7	26.8
1935	52,870	10,610	20.1	24.8
1936	53,440	9,030	16.9	20.8
1937	54,000	7,700	14.3	17.4
1938	54,610	10,390	19.0	23.1
1939	55,230	9,480	17.2	20.8
1940	55,640	8,120	14.6	17.6
1941	55,910	5,560	9.9	11.9
1942	56,410	2,660	4.7	5.6
1943	55,540	1,070	1.9	2.3
1944	54,630	670	1.2	1.5
1945	53,860	1,040	1.9	2.3
1946	57,520	2,270	3.9	4.6
1947	60,170	2,140	3.6	4.1
1948	61,440	2,060	3.4	3.9
1949	62,110	3,400	5.5	6.3
1950	63,100	3,140	5.0	5.6

Sources: Data for 1929 to 1946 from "Labor Force, Employment, and Unemployment 1929-39: Estimating Methods," *Monthly Labor Review,* July 1948, Table 1, p. 51. Data for 1947 to 1952 from Bureau of the Census, *Current Population Reports, Annual Report on the Labor Force,* Series P-50, nos. 13, 19, 31, 40, 45.

[a] It may be noted that this level of the civilian labor force is higher than that obtained in the *1950 Census of Population,* used elsewhere in this report.

Appendix Table 17

Percentage Distribution of Duration of Unemployment for the Philadelphia Labor Force 1929-1938

Year	Labor force 16 years of age & over	Duration of Unemployment in Years[a]								Median duration of unemployment in months
		Total unemployed	Under 1	1 & over	1 & under 2	2 & under 3	3 & under 4	4 & under 5	5 & over	
1929	100.0	8.5	7.9	0.6	—	—	—	—	—	6.4
1930	100.0	13.1	12.4	0.7	0.5	0.2	0.0	0.0	0.0	6.4
1931	100.0	23.6	19.2	4.4	3.4	0.6	0.2	0.1	0.1	7.4
1932	100.0	40.7	26.2	14.5	10.7	2.7	0.7	0.2	0.2	9.3
1933	100.0	44.8	20.2	24.6	14.5	7.1	2.0	0.6	0.4	13.8
1934	100.0	36.1	12.3	23.8	8.2	7.3	4.5	2.4	1.4	20.4
1935	100.0	33.2	11.4	21.8	6.4	5.2	4.2	3.0	3.0	21.7
1936	100.0	29.8	11.8	18.0	5.0	3.5	2.9	2.4	4.2	19.6
1937	100.0	24.2	10.1	14.1	3.8	2.6	1.9	1.6	4.2	18.2
1938	100.0	32.4	15.9	16.5	5.3	3.5	2.2	1.4	4.1	12.6

Source: Industrial Research Department sample surveys.

[a] As measured from date of loss of last job at usual occupation from 1929 to 1934 and from last nonrelief job lasting 1 month or more from 1935 to 1938.

Appendix Table 18

PER CENT OF EXPERIENCED UNEMPLOYED OUT OF WORK ONE YEAR OR OVER, BY AGE PHILADELPHIA, 1932-1938

Age in years	1932	1933	1934[a]	1935[b]	1936	1937	1938
Total	35.5	55.6	68.5	67.6	61.1	58.1	47.2
16—19	20.9	32.5	——	37.5	23.8	13.6	19.5
20—24	31.6	51.4	——	57.9	46.6	38.3	32.2
25—34	34.9	54.1	——	67.8	60.3	57.1	45.9
35—44	36.4	58.5	——	69.4	66.6	66.9	52.9
45—54	41.3	63.7	——	75.3	71.0	70.7	56.2
55—64	52.2	67.9	——	80.1	75.6	75.0	63.1
65 & over	59.7	75.3	——	84.5	80.9	79.5	68.1
Median age of persons unemployed							
1 year or over	35.6	36.4	——	37.9	39.1	40.3	39.4
Under 1 year	30.9	30.9	——	31.3	30.7	29.8	31.5

Source: Industrial Research Department sample surveys.
See footnote to Appendix Table 17.

[a] Not available by age.

[b] Unadjusted for persons not at work because of temporary illness.

For Appendix Table 19 see pages 168 and 169.

Appendix Table 19

Selected Labor Market Indicators for Philadelphia, 1921-1953 (1947-1949=100)

Year	Estimates of help-wanted advertising linage[a]		Placements made by public employment offices[b]		Employment certificates issued to minors[c]		Factory employment[d]	Gross average hourly earnings of factory workers[d]		Average hours worked per week by factory workers[d]		Estimated man-days lost from strikes[e]		Monthly average of compensable unemployment claims[f]	
	No. in 000's	Index	No. in 000's	Index	No. in 000's	Index	Index	$	Index	Number	Index	No. in 000's	Index	No. in 000's	Index
1921					13	81									
1922					16	100									
1923	2,514	117			23	144	103								
1924	1,320	61			17	106	85								
1925	1,751	81	26	52	21	131	94								
1926	1,956	91	25	50	23	144	97								
1927	1,260	59	18	36	21	131	93	.58	42	46.7	117	71	15		
1928	1,139	53	15	30	19	119	90	.58	42	45.5	114	19	4		
1929	1,273	59	17	34	22	138	94	.58	42	51.5	129	184	39		
1930	725	34	13	26	14	88	84	.59	43	46.1	116	184	39		
1931	556	26	11	22	8	50	73	.56	41	42.8	107	536	113		
1932	413	19	8	16	4	25	62	.51	37	39.7	99	46	10		
1933	384	18	12	24	1	6	66	.51	37	38.9	97	602	127		
1934	371	17	15	30	n.a.	—	75	.60	44	35.0	88	499	105		
1935	456	21	13	26	2	13	79	.60	44	36.1	90	162	34		
1936	595	28	12	24	5	31	83	.61	45	38.0	95	347	73		
1937	543	25	14	28	6	38	86	.68	50	38.0	95	929	196		
1938	330	15	14	28	4	25	72	.70	51	35.3	88	489	103	151	102
1939	405	19	14	28	5	31	78	.70	51	37.6	94	249	53	112	75
1940	502	23	22	44	5	31	83	.73	53	38.5	96	210	44	110	74
1941	926	43	60	120	16	100	102	.79	58	41.5	104	418	88	57	39
1942	1,773	82	70	140	39	244	121	.93	68	44.5	112	128	27	34	23
1943	3.753	175	82	164	49	306	135	1.05	77	46.2	116	62	13	6	4

Appendix Table 19 (concluded)

Year	Estimates of help-wanted advertising linage[a]		Placements made by public employment offices[b]		Employment certificates issued to minors[c]		Factory employment[d]	Gross average hourly earnings of factory workers[d]		Average hours worked per week by factory workers[d]		Estimated man-days lost from strikes[e]		Monthly average of compensable unemployment claims[f]	
	No. in 000's	Index	No. in 000's	Index	No. in 000's	Index	Index	$	Index	Number	Index	No. in 000's	Index	No. in 000's	Index
1944	3,163	147	162	324	33	206	129	1.13	82	46.2	116	146	31	3	2
1945	3,006	140	146	292	27	169	110	1.13	82	44.1	111	727	154	37	25
1946	2,836	132	41	82	23	144	99	1.16	85	40.7	102	2,440	516	228	153
1947	2,543	118	50	100	19	119	103	1.28	93	40.5	102	417	88	158	106
1948	2,355	110	57	114	17	106	103	1.38	101	40.3	101	679	144	115	77
1949	1,551	72	42	84	12	75	94	1.46	107	39.0	98	324	68	174	116
1950	2,146	100	59	118	13	81	93	1.51	110	40.3	101	356	75	110	74
1951	4,147	193	63	126	19	119	n.a.	n.a.	n.a.	n.a.	n.a.	290	61	74	49
1952	4,879	227	63	126	20	125	n.a.	n.a.	n.a.	n.a.	n.a.	n.a.	n.a.	84	57
1953	4,866	226	76	152	21	131	n.a.	n.a.	n.a.	n.a.	n.a.	n.a.	n.a.	71	47

[a] Estimated annual totals derived from counts of linage for one week in each month of the year appearing in *The Philadelphia Inquirer* (daily and Sunday) and *The Evening Bulletin.*

[b] Annual totals of placements made by local public employment offices, excluding placements of persons under 15 years of age after 1933, placements on jobs specifying relief personnel, and domestic service placements from January 1945 to October 1946. Upper Darby Office placements from 1942 to 1944 are included (not separable). Data from Pennsylvania State Employment Service in Philadelphia County and Philadelphia Junior Employment Service, supplemented by data from the Pennsylvania Bureau of Employment and Unemployment Compensation.

[c] Annual totals of certificates granted to minors, covering 14-15 year olds from 1921 to 1934, 16-17 year olds after that date. Minors granted vacation certificates and minors hired by Federal Government establishments are excluded. Data from Philadelphia Board of Education.

[d] Annual averages for Philadelphia Five-County Area converted from Philadelphia Federal Reserve Bank Index based on 1923 to 1925 average. Data not available for the five-county area after 1950.

[e] Data from United States Bureau of Labor Statistics: Bulletins Nos. 651, 741, 782, 833, 878, 918, 963, 1003, 1035, 1090. Data not available for city after 1950.

[f] Monthly average of compensable claims under the Unemployment Compensation, Servicemen's Readjustment Allowance and Veterans' Unemployment Compensation programs. Data from Philadelphia District and State Offices of the Pennsylvania Bureau of Employment and Unemployment Compensation. Excludes Upper Darby.

Appendix Table 20

LABOR-FORCE STATUS AND INDUSTRY OF EMPLOYMENT PHILADELPHIA AND THE UNITED STATES, 1940, 1945, 1950 (NUMBERS IN THOUSANDS)

Labor-force status and Industry of employment	1940	1945	1950	Percentage change 1940-1950
		Philadelphia		
Noninstitutional population 14 years and over	1,540	1,707	1,611	+ 4.6
Total labor force	884	1,059	891	+ 0.8
Armed forces	3	183	7	+133.3
Civilian labor force	881	876	884	+ 0.3
Employed	707	863	827	+ 17.0
Unemployed	174	13	57	- 67.2
Nonworkers	656	648	720	+ 9.8
Housework	408	449	434	+ 6.4
School	124	95	109	- 12.1
Other	124	104	177	+ 42.7
Total employed[a]	707	863	827	+ 17.0
Construction	35	30	47	+ 34.3
Manufacturing	256	396	296	+ 15.6
Transportation, communications, and utilities	53	65	70	+ 32.1
Wholesale and retail trade	156	155	180	+ 15.4
Finance, business, and professional services	105	97	125	+ 19.0
Personal services, entertainment	74	62	66	- 10.8
Public administration	26	55	41	+ 57.7
Extractive industries	2	3	2	+ 0.0
		United States		
Noninstitutional population 14 years and over	99,920	105,160	110,910	+ 11.0
Total labor force	53,300	64,160	60,054	+ 12.7
Armed forces	280	12,130	982	+250.7
Civilian labor force	53,020	52,030	59,072	+ 11.4
Employed	45.060	51,300	56,239	+ 24.8
Unemployed	7,960	730	2,833	- 64.4
Nonworkers	46,620	41,000	50,856	+ 9.1
Housework	29,550	27,740	32,180	+ 8.9
School	9,660	6,480	8,424	- 12.8
Other	7,410	6,780	10,252	+ 38.4
Total employed[a]	45,060	51,300	56,239	+ 24.8
Construction	2,107	1,670	3,492	+ 65.7
Manufacturing	10,807	16,110	14,796	+ 36.9
Transportation, communications, and utilities	3,160	4,010	4,435	- 40.3
Wholesale and retail trade	7,693	8,230	10,707	+ 39.2
Finance, business, and professional services	5,769	5,690	8,124	+ 40.8
Personal services, entertainment	4,487	4,000	4,104	- 8.5
Public administration	1,420	2,800	2,526	+ 77.9
Extractive industries	9,617	8,790	8,055	- 16.2

Footnotes for Appendix Table 20

Sources: Data for 1940 for Philadelphia have been adjusted to distribute persons who did not report their labor-force status in 1940, and who had been included in the "other" category under nonworkers in the published Census volumes. The methodology follows that used by the Bureau of the Census in making similar revisions of data for the United States, as published *(1940 Census of Population, Estimates of Labor Force, Employment and Unemployment in the United States, 1940 and 1930)*. It has been assumed that the industrial distribution of employed persons would not be affected by the revisions and therefore the new employment total for each sex has been distributed among industries as the unadjusted total was distributed. Reference to Report No. 36, Series PC-5 *(1950 Census of Population, Preliminary Reports)* indicated that the industry groups presented here required no adjustments for comparability with 1950 industry groups. Data for 1940 for the United States are from U.S. Bureau of the Census, *Monthly Report on the Labor Force,* Special Surveys: M.R.L.F. No. 36 (June 16, 1945), and conform to those published in *Estimates of Labor Force, Employment, etc.;* they are, therefore, comparable to adjusted figures for Philadelphia. An additional adjustment of industry of employment was made for the United States by applying to the adjusted total the percentage distribution of 1940 data converted to the 1950 classifications, as published in the *1950 Census of Population.* The Armed Forces figure is unadjusted (rounded to the nearest ten thousand) and the distribution of nonworkers is from an unpublished estimate made by the U.S. Bureau of the Census. Data for May 1945 for Philadelphia are from an unpublished sample survey of the civilian population conducted by the Bureau of the Census and subject to sampling variability. Data for May 1945 for the United States are from U.S. Bureau of the Census *Labor Force Bulletin* No. 6 and unpublished tabulations. They are subject to sampling variability. Data for 1950 for Philadelphia and the United States are compiled from the *1950 Census of Population, General Characteristics.* The total labor force counts differ from those used in Appendix Table 11. It was necessary to derive estimates of the nonworking population enrolled in school. In the case of Philadelphia, these were based on the proportion of persons 14-29 years of age in the Standard Metropolitan Area enrolled in school and not in the labor force and for the United States on data from the 20 per cent sample.

[a] Persons not reporting industry of employment have been distributed proportionately among all nonagricultural industries.

Appendix Table 21

Industry of Employment in 1944 by Labor-Force Status in December 1941
Philadelphia and the United States

(in thousands)

Industry of employment in 1944	Labor-force status in December 1941: Total		Employed in same industrial group		Employed in different industrial group		Unemployed		Nonworkers	
	Number	Per cent	Number	Per cent	Number	Per cent	Number	Per cent	Number	Per cent
	Philadelphia									
Total employed	853	100.0	532	62.4	148	17.3	24	2.8	149	17.5
Munitions manufacturing	239	100.0	112	46.9	77	32.2	8	3.3	42	17.6
Other manufacturing	170	100.0	113	66.5	19	11.2	5	2.9	33	19.4
Transportation, communications, & utilities	65	100.0	44	67.7	11	16.9	1	1.6	9	13.8
Trade	149	100.0	104	69.8	12	8.1	3	2.0	30	20.1
Finance, insurance, business, professional	88	100.0	65	73.8	8	9.1	2	2.3	13	14.8
Domestic & personal services, amusement & recreation	59	100.0	43	72.9	3	5.1	2	3.4	11	18.6
Other nonmanufacturing	83	100.0	51	61.5	18	21.7	3	3.6	11	13.2

Appendix Table 21 (concluded)

Industry of employment in 1944	Labor-force status in December 1941: Total		Employed in same industrial group		Employed in different industrial group		Unemployed		Nonworkers	
	Number	Per cent	Number	Per cent	Number	Per cent	Number	Per cent	Number	Per cent
	United States									
Total employed	50,491	100.0	32,468	64.3	7,806	15.5	964	1.9	9,253	18.3
Munitions manufacturing	10,107	100.0	4,903	48.5	3,055	30.2	278	2.8	1,871	18.5
Other manufacturing	7,292	100.0	4,633	63.5	925	12.7	194	2.7	1,540	21.1
Transportation, communications, & utilities	4,057	100.0	2,843	70.1	699	17.2	70	1.7	445	11.0
Trade	7,744	100.0	4,972	64.2	745	9.6	122	1.6	1,905	24.6
Finance, insurance, business, professional	5,506	100.0	3,861	70.1	587	10.7	61	1.1	997	18.1
Domestic & personal services, amusement & recreation	3,735	100.0	2,423	64.9	317	8.5	45	1.2	950	25.4
Other nonmanufacturing	12,050	100.0	8,833	73.3	1,478	12.3	194	1.6	1,545	12.8

Source: Data for Philadelphia from unpublished tabulations of May 1944 survey made by the Industrial Research Department in cooperation with the U.S. Bureau of the Census. Data for United States from the U.S. Bureau of the Census, *Current Population Reports, Series* P-50, No. 1, Table A and unpublished tabulations.

Appendix Table 22

Type of Employer Shift, 1940-1949, by Workers' Occupation Group in 1950 and Sex Philadelphia

Occupation group of longest job held in 1950	Type of employer shift and sex of worker					
	Total shifts[a]		Employer only	Employer and occupation	Employer and industry	Employer, occupation, and industry
	Number (in 000's)	Percentage Distribution				
	Men					
All occupations	659	100	15	5	19	61
Professional workers	32	100	19	12	19	50
Managerial workers	75	100	13	15	17	55
Clerical workers	46	100	7	7	17	69
Sales workers	41	100	15	5	19	61
Craftsmen	153	100	23	5	18	54
Operatives	181	100	12	2	22	64
Service workers	61	100	11	3	11	75
Laborers	70	100	19	1	20	60
	Women					
All occupations	221	100	24	4	28	44
Professional workers	17	100	29	6	41	24
Managerial workers	9	100	33	11	11	45
Clerical workers	54	100	9	5	43	43
Sales workers	14	100	22	14	14	50
Craftsmen	3	*	—	—	—	—
Operatives	84	100	32	1	29	38
Service workers	38	100	26	5	11	58
Laborers	2	*	—	—	—	—

Source: Gladys L. Palmer, *Labor Mobility in Six Cities* (New York: Social Science Research Council, 1954), pp. 68-69, 74-75, and unpublished data.

[a] Excludes job shifts not involving a change of employer and those for which occupation was not reported or for which the number of employers was not ascertainable. Occupational and industrial shifts were so counted, if they involved the application of a different code among 269 occupation items and 146 industry items in the classification of the U. S. Bureau of the Census.

* Base too small for presentation of percentages.

Appendix Table 23

Degree and Character of Mobility, 1925-1936 and 1940-1949, for Male Factory Workers 25 Years of Age or Over in 1936 and 1951, Respectively Philadelphia

Selected characteristics of workers and their mobility experience over a decade	Employed in selected factory occupations in 1936[a]	Employed in manufacturing in 1950[b]
Total covered (unweighted)	1637	602
Median age at date of study	40.4	42.3
Per cent skilled craftsmen at date of study	48.3	13.3
Per cent entered labor force during previous decade	6.7	11.0
Per cent migrated to city during previous decade	10.8	12.0
Average job separations[c] per worker in previous decade	3.1	3.8
Average job shifts[d] per worker in previous decade	2.2	1.2
Average employer shifts[d] per worker in previous decade	2.0	1.2
Percentage distribution of employer shifts	100	100
Employer only[d]	30	12
Employer and occupation[e]	5	4
Employer and industry[e]	21	25
Employer, occupation, and industry[e]	44	59

[a] Includes men 25 years of age or over in all occupations in the radio industry, full-fashioned hosiery knitters and helpers, weavers and loomfixers in upholstery, carpet and woolen industries, and machinists and toolmakers in a wide range of industries. Data for workers 16 years of age and over in these studies are summarized in Chapter IV and references cited.

[b] Unpublished data for Philadelphia from the Survey of Patterns and Factors in Labor Mobility, 1940-1950, which was summarized in Gladys L. Palmer, *Labor Mobility in Six Cities* (New York: Social Science Research Council, 1954).

[c] Involving a break of one month or more in the work record for the decade.

[d] In both studies, the records were condensed for casual jobs involving no change of occupation. The counts of job and employer shifts are therefore understated in both studies.

[e] Changes of occupation and industry were so counted if they involved the application of a different code among 343 occupation and 193 industry items from 1925 to 1936 and among 269 occupation and 146 industry items from 1940 to 1949.

Technical Appendix

Derivation of Estimates of Employment in 1910

APPENDIX TABLES A AND B present estimates of employment in 1910 and 1950 by occupation and industry groups. Extensive adjustment of the data for 1910[1] were necessary to secure comparability with data for 1950. The assumptions underlying these adjustments and the methodology followed are outlined below. Because of the prevalence of high levels of employment in 1910, it was assumed that the count of gainful workers (after adjustments for coverage) was the equivalent of the experienced labor force, as measured in 1950. The following adjustments were made for comparability of coverage:

(1) To secure comparable age groups, the data for boys and girls 10-13 years of age were subtracted from the occupational and industrial distributions of all gainful workers, as originally published for the nation and as obtained from unpublished tabulations for the city.

(2) To offset the effect of an estimated overcount of agricultural workers, the national data for laborers in agriculture were adjusted, by use of the methodolgy suggested by Alba M. Edwards in *Comparative Occupation Statistics for the United States, 1870-1940* (16th Census of Population, 1940, Appendix A, p. 137).

Estimates of unemployment by industry for the nation were derived from an unpublished tabulation of unemployed wage and salary workers, 16 years of age and over, by occupation. Over half of the 1910 occupational titles were peculiar to specific industries.

[1] Basic data for the United States are from the *1910 Census of Population*, Vol. IV, Table VI, pp. 302 ff. A parallel table for Philadelphia was made available by the U. S. Bureau of the Census from an unpublished tabulation. Data for 1950 are from the *1950 Census of Population, Detailed Characteristics.*

However, for those occupations that occurred in two or more industries, it was assumed that the industrial distribution of the unemployed would be the same as that for gainful workers. The estimates of the unemployed by industry, so derived, were subtracted from the distribution of gainful workers (adjusted for coverage) to secure estimates of employment by industry. Parallel data for the city were obtained by application of national rates of unemployment by occupation. While the assumptions used in this step might distort the accuracy of estimated unemployment in specific industries, there is every reason to believe it would introduce no bias in employment trends by broad industrial groups from 1910 to 1950.

The estimates of employment, so derived, were in the form of the detailed occupational and industrial titles used in the 1910 Census of Population. These data for the city and the nation were rearranged according to the major occupational and detailed industrial group titles used in 1940. The procedures used for this allocation followed, in modified form, those suggested in Edwards (*op. cit.*, Part I) and were supplemented by suggestions from qualified technicians in the Census Bureau, when estimates had to be made to take account of changes in the title content of specific categories. The national data according to these categories were published in *Industrial and Occupational Trends in National Employment* (Industrial Research Department, University of Pennsylvania, Research Report No. 11) with a detailed discussion of the methodological problems involved.

The 1910 estimates in terms of the major groups used in 1940 were then converted to the 1950 groups by transferring a limited number of specific items which had been changed from one major group to another between 1940 and 1950. A detailed statement of the effect of 1950 code changes on national and state data for 1940, prepared in the Bureau of the Census, provided a guide to the categories affected and the extent of the changes from 1940 levels. However, we made no attempt to prepare detailed estimates for 1910 in the occupational and industrial categories of the 1950 codes. The specific changes that were made to secure greater comparability of national data for 1910 with those for 1950 were duplicated for the city. It should be noted, however, that the figures provided by this roundabout process must be regarded as providing only a "rough" conversion adjustment, for which the Bureau of the Census has no responsibility.

A preliminary version of the 1910 estimates for the United States was published in Palmer and Miller, "The Occupational and Industrial Distribution of Employment, 1910-50" in *Manpower in the United States* (New York: Harper & Brothers, 1954, Chapter VI). The national estimates presented in this report differ slightly from the preliminary estimates because more data upon which to base the conversion pattern have become available in the meantime.

It may be noted that the method of coding occupational information in 1910 did not separate the coding of place of employment, as distinct from type of work, for all occupations (as was done in 1940 and 1950). Difficulties were encountered in recapitulating some categories and the estimates presented here tend to understate the number of workers in business and repair services, and overstate those in personal and professional service industries in 1910. For other reasons, there is an estimated understatement of approximately 15,000 persons in the professional occupations in the nation in 1910. See Research Report No. 11 (pp. 34-37) for further details.

Technical Appendix Table A

Employment by Industry Group,[a] Philadelphia and the United States 1910 and 1950

Industry group	Philadelphia				United States			
	1910		1950		1910		1950	
	Total	Women	Total	Women	Total	Women	Total	Women
All industries[b]	683,958	193,826	827,636	274,305	24,587,053	6,041,403	49,349,539	15,131,020
Manufacturing	270,009	70,604	295,740	93,709	7,279,011	1,330,456	14,817,544	3,721,980
Food and kindred products	14,509	2,242	27,489	7,414	487,637	63,572	1,424,661	325,321
Tobacco manufactures	5,566	2,468	5,233	4,083	186,233	76,567	95,923	50,890
Textile mill products[c]	62,509	30,475	37,241	17,205	870,565	404,428	1,330,853	583,045
Apparel and accessories[c]	34,710	15,026	41,187	25,168	586,383	271,613	1,019,778	728,369
Lumber and wood products, furniture and fixtures	8,969	483	7,047	846	890,806	22,526	1,209,530	92,657
Paper and allied products	5,678	2,500	10,156	3,406	129,407	36,527	474,280	111,926
Printing, publishing, and allied industries	17,725	4,151	21,588	5,754	376,138	76,257	873,529	218,960
Chemicals and allied products, petroleum and coal products	8,799	1,729	19,924	3,969	178,171	27,099	961,771	164,605
Leather and leather products	11,197	2,109	7,304	2,284	334,491	81,422	394,881	175,177
Metal industries, etc.[d]	66,878	3,036	101,012	17,760	1,952,593	106,829	5,730,511	916,301
Other manufacturing[e]	33,469	6,385	17,559	5,820	1,286,587	163,616	1,301,827	354,729

Technical Appendix Table A
(concluded)

Industry group	Philadelphia				United States			
	1910		1950		1910		1950	
	Total	Women	Total	Women	Total	Women	Total	Women
Nonmanufacturing	413,949	123,222	531,896	180,596	17,308,042	4,710,947	34,531,995	11,409,040
Extractive industries[a]	6,952	168	2,160	219	1,092,718	2,876	1,065,838	29,317
Construction	45,682	355	47,028	1,651	2,177,790	8,354	3,493,674	100,659
Transportation, communications, and other public utilities	64,000	2,865	70,675	11,995	3,076,212	134,857	4,439,876	696,456
Transportation	53,839	588	50,322	4,036	2,653,322	32,518	2,986,242	198,638
Telecommunications, utilities, and sanitary services	10,161	2,277	20,353	7,959	422,890	102,339	1,453,634	497,818
Wholesale and retail trade	126,983	28,629	180,062	58,661	4,170,198	810,405	10,735,439	3,629,873
Finance, insurance, and real estate	17,036	3,039	36,475	16,318	584,585	79,327	1,949,961	797,735
Business and repair services	5,039	95	21,099	3,296	278,366	1,978	1,435,713	186,784
Personal sevices	91,352	71,128	58,831	39,088	3,491,497	2,804,460	3,556,773	2,380,521
Entertainment and recreational services	4,763	897	6,891	1,908	174,838	34,027	562,182	144,349
Professional and related services	33,993	14,984	67,118	38,771	1,676,346	788,087	4,761,067	2,776,783
Public administration	18,149	1,062	41,557	8,689	585,492	46,576	2,531,472	666,563

[a] Excluding persons employed in agriculture in the United States.
[b] Persons not reporting industry of employment have been distributed proportionately among all nonagricultural industries.
[c] "Miscellaneous fabricated textile products" are included under "textile mill products" and "hats, except cloth and millinery" are included under "apparel and accessories."
[d] Includes metal industries, machinery and supplies, transportation, professional, and photographic equipment, and watches.
[e] "Other manufacturing" includes "rubber products," "stone, clay, and glass products," "miscellaneous manufacturing industries (durable)," and "not specified manufacturing industries."

Technical Appendix Table B

Employment by Occupation Group
Philadelphia and the United States, 1910 and 1950

Occupation group	1910			1950		
	Total	Men	Women	Total	Men	Women
			Philadelphia			
All occupations	683,958	490,132	193,826	827,636	553,331	274,305
Professional, technical, and kindred workers	35,041	22,054	12,987	69,611	42,905	26,706
Managers, officials, and proprietors	66,312	57,858	8,454	67,615	59,003	8,612
Clerical and kindred workers	73,984	50,250	23,734	133,959	53,310	80,649
Sales workers	42,465	32,543	9,922	61,551	42,615	18,936
Craftsmen, foremen, and kindred workers	119,142	114,429	4,713	127,064	121,417	5,647
Operatives and kindred workers[a]	179,294	104,923	74,371	215,861	137,291	78,570
Service workers	92,563	34,368	58,195	103,972	50,897	53,075
Laborers	75,157	73,707	1,450	48,003	45,893	2,110
			United States			
All nonfarm occupations	24,595,606	18,553,554	6,042,052	49,519,293	34,369,836	15,149,457
Professional, technical, and kindred workers	1,642,564	943,290	699,274	4,909,241	2,970,256	1,938,985
Managers, officials, and proprietors	2,497,215	2,260,963	236,252	5,017,465	4,340,687	676,778
Clerical and kindred workers	1,952,128	1,283,200	668,928	6,894,374	2,602,610	4,291,764
Sales workers	1,827,043	1,446,291	380,752	3,926,510	2,596,786	1,329,724
Craftsmen, foremen, and kindred workers	4,140,300	4,033,160	107,140	7,772,560	7,537,016	235,544
Operatives and kindred workers[a]	5,017,772	3,477,235	1,540,537	11,886,742	8,585,662	3,301,080
Service workers	3,391,521	1,083,118	2,308,403	5,695,169	2,446,566	3,248,603
Laborers	4,127,063	4,026,297	100,766	3,417,232	3,290,253	126,979

[a] For 1950, persons not reporting occupation have been allocated to "operatives and kindred workers" for comparability with 1910.

Bibliographical Appendix

THIS LIST OF SELECTED STUDIES, informal reports, and articles comprises the bulk of the published results of the Industrial Research Department's work in the field of labor-market research. Unless otherwise indicated, all works listed were published by the University of Pennsylvania, the research studies by the University Press, and the releases, monographs, and research reports by the Industrial Research Department. Reports designated P— were issued in cooperation with the Work Projects Administration, National Research Project.

Bezanson, Anne, *et al.*, "A Study in Labor Mobility," Supplement to the *Annals of the American Academy of Political and Social Science,* Vol. CIII, September 1922.

———, *et al.*, "Attendance in Four Textile Mills in Philadelphia," Supplement to the *Annals of the American Academy of Political and Social Science,* Vol. CIV, November 1922.

———, *et al.*, "Four Years of Labor Mobility," Supplement to the *Annals of the American Academy of Political and Social Science,* Vol. CXIX, May 1925.

———, "Labor Market Comparisons—Turnover Rates in Four Metal Manufacturing Centers." *Journal of Personnel Research,* Vol. V, February 1927.

———,*Help-Wanted Advertising as an Indicator of the Demand for Labor,* Industrial Research Study No. 6, 1929. Out of print.

Clague, Ewan, and Webster Powell, *Ten Thousand Out of Work,* Industrial Research Study No. 22, 1933.

Dewhurst, J. Frederic, and Ernest A. Tupper, *Social and Economic Character of Unemployment in Philadelphia, April, 1929,* Bulletin No. 520, United States Bureau of Labor Statistics, 1930.

———, and Robert R. Nathan, *Social and Economic Character of Unemployment in Philadelphia, April, 1930,* Bulletin No. 555, United States Bureau of Labor Statistics, 1932.

de Schweinitz, Dorothea, *How Workers Find Jobs—A Study of Four Thousand Hosiery Workers,* Industrial Research Study No. 15, 1932.

Elderton, Marion, ed., *Case Studies of Unemployment*—Compiled by the Unemployment Committee of the National Federation of Settlements, Industrial Research Study No. 12, 1931.

Loucks, William N., *The Stabilization of Employment in Philadelphia through the Long-Range Planning of Municipal Improvement Projects,* Industrial Research Study No. 15, 1931.

Palmer, Gladys L., *Depression Jobs—A Study of Job Openings in the Philadelphia Employment Office, 1932-1933,* Release No. A-1, 1934. Out of print.

———, *Is the Average Unemployed Worker "Employable"?* Release No. A-2, 1934.

———, *The Applicants at Three Pennsylvania State Employment Offices in 1933,* Release No. A-3, 1934.

———, *The Unemployed in Philadelphia in 1933,* Release No. A-4, 1935.

———, *Trends in the Philadelphia Labor Market in 1934,* Release No. A-5, 1935.

———, *The Employment Characteristics of New Applicants at the Philadelphia State Employment Office, 1934,* Release No. A-6, 1935.

———, *The Incidence and Duration of Unemployment among New Applicants, Philadelphia State Employment Office, 1934*, Release No. A-7, 1936.

———, *Recent Trends in Employment and Unemployment in Philadelphia*, Report No. P-1, 1937.

———, and Ada M. Stoflet, *The Labor Force of the Philadelphia Radio Industry in 1936*, Report No. P-2, 1938.

———, *Employment and Unemployment in Philadelphia in 1936 and 1937*, Report No. P-3, 1938.

———, *et al.*, *Ten Years of Work Experience of Philadelphia Weavers and Loom Fixers*, Report No. P-4, 1938.

———, assisted by Samuel M. Cohn, *Employment and Unemployment in Philadelphia, July-August, 1938*, Release No. 7, 1939.

———, and Janet H. Lewis, *The Long-Term Unemployed in Philadelphia in 1936*, Report No. P-8, 1939.

———, and Constance Williams with the assistance of Valda Noll, *Reemployment of Philadelphia Hosiery Workers after Shut-Downs*, Report No. P-6, 1939.

———, *The Search for Work in Philadelphia, 1932-36*, Report No. P-7, 1939.

———, "Some Considerations Involved in Appraising the Adequacy of Occupational Statistics," *Journal of the American Statistical Association*, Vol. 36, March 1941.

———, "The Mobility of Weavers in Three Textile Centers," *The Quarterly Journal of Economics*, Vol. LVI, May 1941.

———, assisted by Samuel M. Cohn, *War Labor Supply Problems of Philadelphia and Its Environs*, Industrial Research Report No. 5, 1942.

———, *The Significance of Employment Patterns in Households for Labor Market Analysis*, Release No. 8, 1942.

———, assisted by Sophie T. Cambria, *The Manpower Outlook in Philadelphia in 1943*, Industrial Research Report No. 7, 1943.

———, "Factors in the Variability of Response in Enumerative Studies," *Journal of the American Statistical Association*, Vol. 38, June 1943.

———, assisted by Ann Ratner, *The Philadelphia Labor Market in 1944*, Industrial Research Report No. 8, 1944. Out of print.

———, and Ann Ratner, *Labor Force and Employment Estimates for Philadelphia and Environs with a Projection for 1950*, Part II of a report to the Philadelphia City Planning Commission from the Population and Economic Research Advisory Committee under the auspices of the Institute of Local and State Government, University of Pennsylvania, 1946.

———, and Ann Ratner, "Use of Population Census Data in the Preparation of Estimates of Labor Force and Employment in a Metropolitan Area," Appendix C of *Labor Force Definition and Measurement*, prepared for the Subcommittee on Labor Force Statistics, Labor Market Research Committee, Social Science Research Council, Bulletin 56, 1947.

———, and Ann Ratner, *Industrial and Occupational Trends in National Employment, 1910-1940, 1910-1948*, Industrial Research Report No. 11, 1949.

———, assisted by June R. Charlamb, *Mobility of Philadelphia Workers, 1940 through 1949*, Informal report, 1951.

———, and Ann Ratner Miller, assisted by Rosamond J. Sanderson, *Work Attachment Patterns in Six Cities*, Informal report, 1953.

———, assisted by Carol P. Brainerd, *Labor Mobility in Six Cities*: A report prepared for the Committee on Labor Market Research of the Social Science Research Council and published by the Council, New York, 1954.

———, and Ann R. Miller, "The Occupational and Industrial Distribution of Employment, 1910-1950," chap. 6 in Haber, *et al.*, *Manpower in the United States: Problems and Policies*, New York: Harper and Brothers, 1954.

Welch, Emmett H., *Employed Married Women in Philadelphia*, Release, 1931. Out of print.

———, *Unemployment in Philadelphia Families, April 1931,* Release No. 1, 1931. Out of print.

———, *Social Characteristics of Unemployment in Philadelphia, April 1931,* Release No. 2, 1932. Out of print.

———, *Duration of Unemployment in Philadelphia, April 1931,* Release No. 3, 1932. Out of print.

———, *Industrial and Occupational Characteristics of Unemployment in Philadelphia, April 1931.* Release No. 4, 1932. Out of print.

———, *Family Conditions in Philadelphia, May 1932,* Release No. 5, 1933.

———, *Unemployment in Philadelphia Families, May 1932,* Release No. 6, 1933.

INDEX

INDUSTRIAL RESEARCH STUDIES

2. *Collective Bargaining among Photo-Engravers in Philadelphia,* by Charles Leese. 1929. $2.50.
3. *Trends in Foundry Production in the Philadelphia Area,* by Anne Bezanson and Robert D. Gray. 1929. $1.50.
5. *Earnings in Certain Standard Machine-Tool Occupations in Philadelphia,* by H. L. Frain. 1929. $1.50.
7. *An Analysis of Production of Worsted Sales Yarn,* by Alfred H. Williams, Martin A. Brumbagh, and Hiram S. Davis. 1929. $2.50.
8. *The Future Movement of Iron Ore and Coal in Relation to the St. Lawrence Waterway,* by Fayette S. Warner. 1930. $3.00.
10. *Wage Methods and Selling Costs,* by Anne Bezanson and Miriam Hussey. 1930. $4.50.
11. *Wages—A Means of Testing Their Adequacy,* by Morris E. Leeds and C. Canby Balderston. 1931. $1.50.
13. *The Full-Fashioned Hosiery Worker—His Changing Economic Status,* by George W. Taylor. 1931. $3.00
16. *How Workers Find Jobs—A Study of Four Thousand Hosiery Workers,* by Dorothea de Schweinitz. 1932. $2.50.
17. *Savings and Employee Savings Plan,* by William J. Carson. 1932. $2.50.
19. *Union Tactics and Economic Change—A Case Study of Three Philadelphia Textile Unions,* by Gladys L. Palmer. 1932. $2.00.
20. *The Philadelphia Upholstery Weaving Industry,* by C. Canby Balderston, Robert P. Brecht, Miriam Hussey, Gladys L. Palmer, and Edward N. Wright. 1932. $2.50.
21. *Wage Rates and Working Time in the Bituminous Coal Industry, 1912-1922,* by Waldo E. Fisher and Anne Bezanson. 1932. $3.50.
22. *Ten Thousand Out of Work,* by Ewan Clague and Webster Powell. 1933. $2.00.
25. *Executive Guidance of Industrial Relations,* by C. Canby Balderston, 1935. $3.75.
26. *Prices in Colonial Pennsylvania,* by Anne Bezanson, Robert D. Gray, and Miriam Hussey. 1935. $4.00.
27. *Earnings of Skilled Workers in a Manufacturing Enterprise, 1878-1930,* by Evan Benner Alderfer. 1935. $1.50.
28. *Depression and Reconstruction,* by Eleanor Lansing Dulles. 1936. $3.00.
29. *Wholesale Prices in Philadelphia—1784-1861,* by Anne Bezanson, Robert D. Gray, and Miriam Hussey. 1936. $4.00.
30. *Wholesale Prices in Philadelphia—1784-1861, Part II—Series of Relative Monthly Prices,* by Anne Bezanson, Robert D. Gray, and Miriam Hussey. 1937. $4.00.
32. *Economic Consequences of the Seven-Hour Day and Wage Changes in the Bituminous Coal Industry,* by Waldo E. Fisher. 1939. $2.00.
34. *Effective Labor Arbitration,* by Thomas Kennedy. 1948. $3.50.

Limited supplies of the titles listed above are available at
Industrial Research Unit, 3440 Walnut St., Philadelphia 4, Pa.

35. *Prices and Inflation During the American Revolution, Philadelphia, 1770-1790,* by Anne Bezanson. 1951. $6.75.
36. *Wholesale Prices in Philadelphia, 1852-1896 (Tables),* by Anne Bezanson. 1954. $10.00.
37. *Productivity Accounting,* by Hiram S. Davis. 1955. $5.00.

Titles 35, 36, and 37 may be ordered from:

UNIVERSITY OF PENNSYLVANIA PRESS
3436 Walnut Street
Philadelphia 4, Pa.